D0374208

Honest to God
The 10 Questions Jews Ask Christian Zionists

Pastor Victor L. Styrsky

—————

Forward by:
David Brog/Author
Standing With Israel (FrontLine 2006)
In Defense of Faith (Encounter Books 2012)

Honest to God
The 10 Questions Jews Ask Christian Zionists

Copyright © 2013 by Pastor Victor L. Styrsky

Cover Art: *The Crusaders*, by Elizabeth Hoskinson
FineArtAmerica.com/profiles/Elizabeth-hoskinson.html

Cover design: Kate Styrsky

All rights reserved. No part of this book may be reproduced or transmitted in any form or by any means without written permission from the author.

ISBN 978-0-9888546-0-4

Printed in USA

First published as *Honest to God: Christian Zionists Confront 10 Questions Jews Need Answered*
Artzy Books, Devora Publishing 2009
ISBN 978-1-934440-49-0

Go to www.cufi.org to join in our efforts to strengthen United States support of Israel

You may contact Pastor Victor at:
victor@cufi.org

"What can I say? I have to hold back tears to read your words. I have never heard nor read anything like it in my life. It is difficult to describe what it means to me as a Jewess. I'm sure you have heard it from others. I feel overwhelmed by the deepest emotions, as though it is not just me receiving your numinous gifts; there is a welling up of something that is more than just me, in my blood my ancestors singing in relief, gratitude and joy."

Carla Stang - Sydney, Australia

"This book is one of the best books I have read in the past two or three years! Informative, enlightening, and convicting....you will not want to put this book down for very long."

Pastor F. Victa - Nashua, NH

"-- read your book yesterday as I was flying to Atlanta and returning home last night. It is excellent -- very well stated, direct and unambiguous. It's written as if you and I were sitting discussing all of the topics over a cup of coffee. I hope it gets wide distribution. The guy sitting next to me on the plane couldn't figure out why I was either smiling and/or shedding a few tears -- he should read the book too!"

L Wunsch - President & CEO / Jewish Federation of Houston

"I went to the CUFI DC Summit, incredible time and read your book all the way home, finished and bought two more copies, buying more to give to college friends of my daughter. Loved the book...my husband is now reading it, no matter what your faith may be this answers many questions I've had...thank you, Shalom!!"

Pastor M. Roseberg -Atlanta, GA

"I was going to write a longer letter after I finished your amazing book. Still awaiting down time to do that. I will pass the book on when I finish. It's a must read for our people. My anger at Christianity has waned and almost disappeared thanks to you..."

M. Long - Founder/ Christians and Jews United for Israel

"*In reading Pastor Styrsky's book* Honest to G-d, *I was moved not only by his deep-rooted love of Israel but his ability to inspire our community, the Jewish people, to our historic role and responsibility in supporting the State of Israel with courage and conviction.*"

Rabbi Daniel Cohen
Congregation Agudath Sholom
The largest Modern Orthodox congregation in New England

"*Here, Styrsky tackles the questions that the Jewish Community demands from Christian Zionists in a manner that is articulate, sensitive and no-holds-barred. A must for anyone wishing to understand the true reasons that many Christians love Israel and the Jewish people so dearly.*"

Amazon Books Review

"Your book is amazing and your love of the Jewish people is apparent in every page! I couldn't put it down while reading it and I have recommended it to my friends!"
Carole Simon, CA

"If you love Israel you must get the book **Honest to God**. A tremendous resource for all those who desire to stand with Israel and our Jewish friends with truth and knowledge."
Pastor D. Livingston – Pensacola, FL

A Wonderful Surprise . . .

My *Honest to God* book project has been a blessing for me to write and a blessing for some who have read it as well. I can't tell you how many folks come up to me and tell me stories concerning the impact it has had on their lives and upon those to whom they have passed it on. The thought, that my thoughts may have inspired others is encouraging, surprising, and truly humbling to me.

While in Washington, D.C., I was approached by a man from Florida who "just had to tell me a story" about *Honest to God.*

"I was waiting to get on a plane a few weeks ago, and was conversing with a woman who was also seated at the gate," he began.

"We spoke for about 30 minutes before they finally called us to board. As we did so, we both laughed, finding that we would be sitting right next to each other on the plane! We continued our conversation and as it grew ever more personal, my new friend was now weeping as she told a heartbreaking story of her 23-year marriage that had just ended in divorce."

Making matters nearly unbearably worse, her former pastor and church fellowship were now shunning her.

The nightmarish tale continued, as did the tears while she grieved over her three grown children who also had cut off all communication from her due to their religious views concerning divorce.

"I've been re-reading your book *Honest to God* and happened to have it with me so I put it in her hand and told her, "You have got to read the prologue to this book right now!'" he continued.

"I ended up giving her the book - and I just received an email from her *today* on my way here to DC," my friend informed me as he then read the following:

"I begged my children, and my former pastor to read the prologue of Honest to God - *and we are now re-united and in the process of healing! "*

"She also wanted me to tell you that the rest of the book moved her as well!" he laughed.

This is the third person I have heard about whose life after divorce was changed by the prologue of this book.

What a wonderful and unexpected surprise for me.

At the end of this "Revised and Updated" printing of *Honest to God*, you will find the opening chapter to my new book, *Jews, Gentiles, and the World to Come!* Available - God willing in the summer of 2013

I sincerely thank you for your desire to explore my thoughts concerning *The 10 Questions Jews Ask Christian Zionists*. I truly hope you enjoy the prologue . . . and the rest of the book too!

-- Victor

~ This book is dedicated to my magnificent father,
Alfred B. Styrsky ~

He rests peacefully and I miss him.

Table of Contents

Foreword 9

Introduction 13

Prologue 28

Question 1 37
Does the Christian community have the patience for us?

Question 2 73
Do Christians still hate us because we don't believe in Jesus?

Chapter 3 91
What is your real agenda in reaching out to the Jews?

Chapter 4 109
What can we do about Christians who target us and our children?

Chapter 5 127
Why Don't You Educate the Anti-Israel Churches?

Chapter 6 155
How are Christian Zionists trying to influence Israeli politics?

Chapter 7 193
Do you really believe all the Jews are going to hell?

Chapter 8 215
You love your enemies? How can you love the terrorists who are killing our children in Israel?

Chapter 9 257
What would you say if a Jew told you he wanted to convert to Christianity?

Chapter 10 273
What is your deepest prayer for the Jewish people?

Introduction 283
Jews, Gentiles, and the World to Come!

Resources 289

Foreword

by David Brog (2009)

In the early years of this decade, I worked for Senator Arlen Specter as his Chief Counsel and, later, his Chief of Staff. Senator Specter represents Pennsylvania, a state with a significant Jewish community largely concentrated in the urban areas of Philadelphia and Pittsburgh. It is also a state with a large and vibrant evangelical Christian community spread throughout the smaller cities and rural communities of the state's middle section.

Over the years, I noticed an extremely interesting phenomenon.

Whenever there would be a terrorist attack in Israel, or an anti-Semitic incident in Europe, my phone would light up with calls from constituents back in Pennsylvania. But to my surprise, a majority of these calls came not from our Jewish constituents in the cities, but from our Christian constituents in the middle of the state. These evangelical Christians were upset that Jewish blood was being spilled, and they wanted Senator Specter to do something about it. There was no mistaking the sincerity and depth of their concern.

As a Jew raised in the Northeast, however, I had what I have come to learn is a typical reaction to this outpouring of Christian concern: I was immediately suspicious. Throughout our long and often tragic history, we Jews have not always been well loved by our Gentile neighbors. As a result, we have developed a deep-seated skepticism (bordering on paranoia) when it comes to their intentions. Unable to believe that Christians would support us out of love or solidarity, we search for their "ulterior motive." And if no such ulterior motive exists, we invent one. In Jewish and secular circles, an absurd conventional wisdom maintains that evangelicals support Israel only to convert Jews now or to speed an Armageddon, which will bring our ultimate conversion or destruction.

Yet something about these cynical explanations for Christian support simply didn't ring true to me. These dark motives did not match the sincerity and love that I had seen in the eyes and heard in the voices of so many Christian friends. It seemed to me that there had to be more to the story.

Thus I began the research that formed the basis of my book **Standing with Israel.** As I learned more about the topic, it became increasingly clear to me that the conventional wisdom about Christian support for Israel was an urban myth, without any connection to the truth. Having been the victims of so many slanders about our own faith, we Jews must do better than to passively accept such slanders when they are made against others. Far from wanting to speed our demise, evangelical Christians who stand with Israel today are nothing less than the theological heirs of the religious righteous gentiles who risked their lives to save Jews from the Holocaust.

After writing my book, I was intellectually convinced that evangelical Christians are real and sincere friends without ulterior motive. But I must confess that my heart had not kept up with nmy head. After having grown up with so much suspicion, I did not quickly let my guard down. It was with tense shoulders and crossed arms that I spoke to actual Christian Zionists.

Then I met Pastor Victor Styrsky. We appeared together on a panel at a pro-Israel conference. Here in front of me was a flesh-and-blood example of the latter-day righteous Gentile I had written about in my book. Here was a man who was visibly pained by the history of Christian anti-Semitism that he knew so well. Here was a man who wanted not only to mourn the tragedies of the past but to change the future. Here was a man who felt a dedication to the Jewish people and Israel every bit as emotional, deep, and real as my own.

It did not take long until we had recruited Victor into the leadership of Christians United for Israel. But even more importantly, it did not take long until Victor had become one of my dearest friends and closest brothers. It is hard to maintain psychological distance when someone shares your heart. Victor was one of my first personal connections in the Christian world, and through Victor I have come to make so many more.

I therefore am thrilled that Victor has finally put pen to paper and shared his warm and oversized heart with a broader audience. It is one thing for me, a Jew, to describe what motivates Christian support for Israel. It is quite another thing for a Christian supporter of Israel to share his beliefs and thoughts directly. This book is a valuable contribution to what is still a far too limited literature.

I strongly encourage my fellow Jews to take the time to read this book. Throughout all of the lonely centuries, we have prayed for more understanding, appreciation and love from our Gentile neighbors. Today, in America, this prayer has been answered in so many ways, including the rise of millions of pro-Israel Christians. Before we dismiss this outpouring of support on the basis of myths and misinformation, we must at least give our friends a hearing, and make an effort to understand them. Victor Styrsky has saved you the trouble of trying to piece together the thinking of Christian Zionists– it is all in his book. Start reading; you might just like what you see.

This book is also a valuable resource for Christians. Supporting Israel and working with the Jewish community is a most challenging enterprise. Religion, politics and a troubled history will place many stumbling blocks in your path. Victor's experience from twenty-five years of pro-Israel work will help clear the way for you. It is a most effective primer.

I must warn you. Victor is harder on his fellow Christians than I would ever be. I have argued that pro-Israel Christians in America today have nothing whatsoever to do with the Christians who persecuted Jews years ago in distant lands. Victor strongly and consistently disagrees with me and assumes responsibility for anti-Semitic acts done in the name of his Savior. I understand that Christians are unfamiliar with Jews and our sensitivities and that it will take time before we have bridged these gaps. Victor is often impatient when Christians unwittingly insult Jewish sensibilities. Yet while I may disagree with Victor's position, I am by no means surprised by it. It is just like Victor to demand more of himself and of his fellow Christians than others would.

We believe that through our work we can bridge an ancient gap and heal a centuries-old wound. We believe that in so doing we bring joy to the God of Abraham, Isaac and Jacob whom we all worship. This journey of Christian and Jewish reconciliation has been one of the most fulfilling and inspiring of my life. I hope you will choose to join us on this journey.

I can think of few better ways of beginning than with the book you are about to read.

Introduction

Thirty Years of Supporting Israel

My decision to write this book is born out of the persistent encouragement of my Jewish and Christian friends. The endeavor results from puzzling and painful discoveries I have made as an evangelical Christian Zionist speaking before many Jewish audiences all around the country.

Through the mysterious way of the Almighty, I have had the distinct privilege of being one of the few evangelical Christians to address Jewish leaders and members of American Israel Public Affairs Committee (AIPAC) at numerous summits and conferences throughout the United States. From synagogues and Jewish homes to student leadership at New York University to University of Texas-Austin campuses, I have preached and listened to, laughed and wept with Jewish audiences as we examine the past, present and future of our two communities.

The people attending these events have consistently posed questions about Christianity's horrific historic abominations. These audiences are equally perplexed by Christian present-day thinking about the Jewish people. Without fail, their feedback includes accounts of the arrogant and ignorant answers they commonly received from well-meaning Christians that confirm their worst and most fearful suspicions concerning Christians. I have been the recipient of numerous excruciating personal narratives from Jews whose religious interchanges with Christians commonly reveal a pattern of dialogue that left my new acquaintances in disbelief, confusion, and outrage.

Astonishing Ignorance Within Christianity

A petite Jewish woman once inquired of me at a parlor meeting on behalf of the American Israel Public Affairs Committee (AIPAC), "Pastor, I know an evangelical Christian who seems to be very nice, and he explained to me that you believe the Jewish children murdered in the Holocaust are now in hell. Is that really what you teach in your churches?"

"He seems to be very nice?" I thought to myself while trying not to curse or cry. Is so little expected of the Christian community by the Jews that simply conversing with them now qualifies as being nice?

In a dreadfully perverse way, perhaps, this Christian was being "nice" by imparting his vicious and ignorant judgment rather than inflicting physical violence in his self-righteous arrogance. Nice when compared to the horrors of our past behavior toward the Jews.

Through painful and illuminating stories from more than twenty-five years of interactions with Jewish people who are dismayed and yet hopeful because of Christian supporters' professed *love* for them, I will examine each of the "10 questions Jews ask Christian Zionists." After exposing the standard and often alarming replies communicated by many members of the Christian community, I then will offer alternative responses that are Biblically sound, compassionate, and comprehensible for our Jewish brethren of the faith.

Not only do I hope to bring an accurate understanding of the emerging Christian Zionist faith to my Jewish readers, but I also hope to dislodge the self-imposed *burden* of preaching the Good News that Christians sometimes drag around with them like a ton of bricks. Believers in the New Testament are promised that the cross of Christ is an easy yoke and light burden; yet we frequently hurl splinter-filled planks upon those who inquire of our convictions. We have a consistent record of that approach throughout our entire history with the Jewish people.

At a wedding reception recently, I sat next to a nominally pro-Israel Christian. During our conversation, I was astonished to hear that the young man had never heard of Europe's pogroms. I hear you asking: How do you start chatting about the pogroms of Europe at a wedding celebration? With my customary fervor, I began reciting the history of the Crusades, the Inquisition, the darkened and anti-Semitic heart of Martin Luther.

The young wedding guest suddenly interrupted me, "Pastor Victor, where are you getting all this stuff?!"

"What do you mean, where am I getting it?" I answered, trying to figure out if he was serious.

"Well," he continued respectfully, "it sounds like an Internet hoax to me."

My wife and I arrived home from that wedding party around midnight, but I immediately went to my Christian friend's house to leave a copy of David Brog's excellent book, "Standing With Israel," on his porch. I wish I could say this type of historic ignorance within the Christian community is uncommon. Astonishingly, it is not.

What Is A Christian Zionist?

Christian Zionist: a member of the Christian faith who believes in the eternal, unconditional Biblical covenants God made with Abraham, Isaac, and Jacob. These promises include the gifting of the land of Israel to the descendents of these Jewish patriarchs.

Christian Zionists do not believe the Jews are illegal occupiers of the land of Israel – we believe they are inheritors of the land of Israel!

Honest to God briefly covers my thirty years as a Christian Zionist through personal experiences of loving the Jewish people, the land of Israel, and the Jewish carpenter from Nazareth who extraordinarily changed and undoubtedly saved my life.

My religious birth began in my rock-and-roll, hippie-commune days of the 1970s and continues with my experiences as an evangelical Christian Zionist and my encounters as the California Director of Christians United For Israel (CUFI).

Yet another unexpected twist in my story is that I-- a pastor and Christian Zionist-- have lived with my family in the midst of a very devout Pakistani Sunni Muslim community in California for over fifteen years. We bought our home completely aware of the religious makeup of the neighborhood. (It is with reverence and an ever-growing appreciation of God's sovereignty in our lives we occasionally refer to Him as *Jehovah Sneaky* – seeing He pretty much does whatever He wants with us!)

In *Honest To God: The 10 Questions Jews Ask Christians Zionists,* I confront the near-irreparable havoc that many well-meaning Christians inflict upon the hearts of God's biblically proclaimed chosen people through superficial and inaccurate rhetoric about our faith as it relates to them as Jews. These chapters contain accounts of Christian Zionism's awakening in the contemporary church, as well as of the church's ongoing apathy and anti-Semitic arrogance toward the Jews and the land of Israel.

The Christian Curse

For over 1,900 years, hordes of those carrying the banner of Christianity have betrayed the Jewish people.

Appallingly betrayed them - over and over and over again.

Betrayed them not only by bankrupt souls in clothes of self-righteous aberration who perpetrated the Crusades and the Inquisition, but also betrayed them by the Christian societies of Spain and Germany, Poland, and much of the rest of the world. After feasting on the fruits of Jewish ingenuity and brilliance brought to countless aspects of living, these anti-Semites, by the darkened reasoning of their collective jealous and wicked hearts, disdainfully cast the Jews out of cities built by their own hands into uninhabitable ghettos or a continued Diaspora.

For My Christian Readers:
Diaspora: the dispersion of Jews outside of Israel from the sixth century B.C., when they were exiled to Babylonia, until the present time. From the Greek *diaspeirein,* "to scatter."

I empathize with the pain, disbelief and fear generated in the hearts of many Jews because of the unrelenting Christian sins committed against them. I feel their anguish as strongly as I feel the peace and strength garnered from the deepest tenets of my Christian faith. These two paradigms battle within me, often pressing me throughout the day, hounding me in the night, and awakening me in the morning. I have touched the still raw wounds, oozing with suspicion and distrust, of Holocaust survivors, rabbis, Jewish college students, Jewish children and their terrified parents, an infection left by years of wickedness from perverse "saints" marching under the banner of Christianity.

The silence of the church during the Holocaust continues to bewilder the Jewish community today; as does the aggressiveness of Christian attempts to convert Jews without showing any apparent awareness or understanding of why conversion is such an abominable concept to them.

I have been afforded an intimate view of these gaping, angry holes in the lives of many precious Jewish people through the friendships I have developed over the years. Only because of the candid questions presented within the privileged sanctity of cautious trust have I glimpsed the sociological mayhem Christians have wreaked between our two communities.

In honesty, I have not always perceived or been moved so deeply over my friends' torment. But I am today. And I remember the journey that has brought me here. I'm determined to gather my Christian brethren to this place, this place of attempting comprehension of the Christian curse that has been cast upon God's firstborn, the children of Abraham, Isaac, and Jacob.

Sins of Our Ancestors - Sins of Our Brothers

A very precious and brilliant Jewish friend repeatedly contends, "Pastor Victor, you evangelical Christians of today have nothing at all in common with those calling themselves Christians during the Crusades, or the Inquisition, or the pogroms of Europe."

I thank him for his kindness, but each time I must and do absolutely disagree.

We are connected to those Christians.

Of course we are. For we too carry the name of the carpenter from Nazareth who has affected our lives in such a remarkable way. We are, by spiritual bloodline, tethered to the rabid insanity

18

spat from the mouth and scratched from the pen of our patriarchal Protestant reformer Martin Luther in his diatribe *On the Jews and Their Lies*. We contemporary Christians are as linked to the deadly cold silence of the American church during the Holocaust as we are to the current disengagement and anti-Semitic ramblings of liberal Christian churches. Former President Jimmy Carter is, by his confirmed "faith in Christ," an anti-Semitic Christian brother and we are all related through and by the name Christians call the Name above all Names.

Through the eyes of many Jews, and by our Christian salvation-through-faith theology, we are connected with those who carry and call upon the Name of Jesus, in the present and in the past. By our confession of faith in Him, we share in the shame of our reprobate brethren and we should feel our own shame for not making the admission.

"But that was the Catholic Church!"
"There were some Christians that helped Jews during WWII!"
"I'm not responsible for what others have done!"

If you are a Christian, and these are your immediate responses, then I implore you to read this book.

Until we embrace the realities of how the Church's failures have exiled the Jewish people from the mercies we have been commanded to extend them, we are not capable of fulfilling God's heart cry to comfort them.

Isaiah 40:1
"Comfort ye, comfort ye My people," saith your God.

Having been a pastor and lived in the church for most of the past thirty-five years, I sadly have found few who believe in or grieve over these realities. Even fewer seem to know much-- if anything at all-- about this atrocious and bloody history of the Church.

My Jewish friends incredulously ask, "Come on, how can someone not know? How can Christians not be aware of the 1,900 years of atrocities executed against us in the name of their Christian savior?! I just can't believe it."

My answer to them on our behalf is embarrassing, shocking, and true: much of the Christian community is woefully ignorant of church history. Pastors don't preach it; congregants don't study it.

The outcome of this willful and pathetic ignorance adds to the rising evidence of our inability to mature as a faith community. To make matters worse, many Christians believe-- by uninformed or misinformed default-- that the history of the Jews ended at the death and resurrection of Christ and that, because of their infidelities as God's chosen people, we Christians have replaced them.

"Really?" I ask. "God grew tired of the Jews' failures, removed His Name from them and placed it exclusively upon us?" I sarcastically intone to my Christian brethren.

"And you think you can make a case that Christians have done better than Jews in obeying the Almighty?" I mock.

Let's consider: "Did God really tire of the Jews and their failures and renege on all the promises He made them?"

The Apostle Paul warns us as he writes to Gentile Christians concerning the mystery within God's eternal love for the Jews:
Romans 11: 1, 25
"I say then, God has not rejected His people, has He? God forbid! May it never be so! ... I do not want you to be ignorant of this mystery, brothers; so that you may not be conceited!"

That you may not be conceited?

Is there any form of conceit more insidious than the unabated persecution of a people solely based upon their not sharing your religious beliefs?

Uncommon Christian Behavior

The Jewish community is well aware of, and forever grateful to, the righteous Gentiles who throughout our sordid Christian history gave their lives to protect Jewish lives. The Jews have built numerous monuments on behalf of these heroes of the faith. History has accurately and permanently recorded the actions of these saints as exhibiting extraordinary-- and as uncommon Christian behavior.

Conceit in the Church Continues

I lost much of my youthful innocence in the world of rock-and-roll. Then, as a pastor for twenty-five years, I was stripped of what naiveté remained by the shock of discovering the sins within the church; the sins recorded throughout our history, the enormity of the sins congregants reveal to their leaders in confidence, and the secret lives of hypocritical pastors. My wife and I writhe in dismay every time one of our national Christian leaders is caught and reported on the news as living a life of pretense. We scream at the television, "YOU'RE KILLIN' US OUT HERE!!" These Christian men, who are exposed for committing the very same sins in the night that they have howled against on Sunday mornings, are by lineage my brothers in Christ.

I scream at them, I share their shame and dismay, I forgive them and I cry for them and their families. I do realize that "there but for the grace of God," and so on. But what a fearful negligence of the church for not stepping up to the local news microphones and declaring to the public, "We are sick, ashamed, and angry over this news. We ask for God's and your forgiveness.

We do love Pastor _____ and ask that you pray for his family, for him, and for our church community."

Humility is not one of the qualities for which the Christian community is known. Yet along with love, humility is supposed to be one of the very basic elements of our faith.

One night we were watching the Larry King Show as one of our most highly esteemed Christian leaders was being interviewed. He was asked regarding a fallen prominent pastor whose homosexual lifestyle the man had been hiding from his wife and family.

"Do you think this was hypocritical of Pastor _____ ?"

King scowled. "No I don't," was the gentle reply. "He had been fighting against these dark impulses for a long– blah, blah, blah," the Christian guest submitted.

We hollered at the television, "Are you kidding me?? The devil made him do it??"

"YOU'RE KILLIN' US OUT HERE!!"

The only honest answer for the matter is, "Yes. Of course he was being hypocritical. Pastor _____'s actions are the epitome of hypocrisy."

Is our Christian faith so frail that admitting our failures is tantamount to the surrender of our convictions? Those observing us may conclude so. In regard to the church's relationship with the Jewish people, this lack of integrity is much more insidious than our grandiose self-righteousness. Centuries of massacring Jews exemplify the supreme incarnation of arrogance. For the Christian reader who is now protesting:

"But we've been forgiven! We have the promises Jesus made to us! WE have His precious promises! We have the New Covenant!"

I answer: "The Jews also have precious promises."

God's Promises to the Jews

The Jewish people have promises made to them by the God of Abraham, Isaac, and Jacob– the God our Jesus called *Abba*. Jesus' Father swore that He would keep these promises with the descendants of children of Israel– forever. One of those promises is in regard to the land of Israel.

Genesis 17:8

"Also I give to you and your descendants after you the land in which you are a stranger, all the land of Canaan, as an everlasting possession; and I will be their God."

For My Christian Readers:
Abba, the Aramaic word for "Father," "my Father," together with its Greek equivalent, occurs three times in the New Testament. It is an invocation to God, reflecting a tender and personal relationship between the speaker and God. There is nothing especially Christian about this. It was the formula for addressing God that was very familiar to the religious Jews of New Testament times.

God promised He would keep the promises forever. Many of these promises were based not on the faithfulness or works of the Jewish people (just like many of His promises to us), but solely based upon His Name, His love for the Jewish people, and His resolve to demonstrate that He is God. He has made and will keep these promises in order to show all the nations of the world that He is God alone, that He is good and that He alone is able to make the Jews a holy people, for they are unable to attain holiness on their own merit. (Just like us Christians.)

Ezekiel 36:22-25

Therefore say unto the house of Israel: Thus saith the Lord God: "I do not this for your sake, O house of Israel, but for My holy Name, which ye have profaned among the nations whither ye came. And I will sanctify My great Name, which hath been profaned among the nations, which ye have profaned in the midst of them; and the nations shall know that I am HaShem," saith the Lord God, "when I shall be sanctified in you before their eyes.

"For I will take you from among the nations, and gather you out of all the countries, and will bring you into your own land. And I will sprinkle clean water upon you, and ye shall be clean; from all your uncleannesses, and from all your idols, will I cleanse you."

For My Christian Readers:

HaShem is a Hebrew word for God, meaning "The Name." Jews use it as a substitute word when referring to God in situations other than prayer or worship. This is done to honor the Almighty and prevent using the Name of God in vain.

"And that 'New Covenant' you're citing?" I continue.

"That New Covenant we're all so proud about – when we're supposed to be humble and broken over it?" I remind my Christian brethren.

"That covenant was first declared by God through the Jewish prophet Jeremiah, and that covenant is a promise made to the Jews," I finish.

24

Jeremiah 31:31-37

"Behold, the days come," saith HaShem, "that I will make a new covenant with the house of Israel, and with the house of Judah; not according to the covenant that I made with their fathers in the day that I took them by the hand to bring them out of the land of Egypt; forasmuch as they broke My covenant, although I was a lord over them," saith HaShem.

"But this is the covenant that I will make with the house of Israel after those days," saith HaShem, "I will put My law in their inward parts, and in their heart will I write it; and I will be their God, and they shall be My people; and they shall teach no more every man his neighbor, and every man his brother, saying: 'Know HaShem;' for they shall all know Me, from the least of them unto the greatest of them," saith HaShem; "for I will forgive their iniquity, and their sin will I remember no more."

Thus saith HaShem, Who giveth the sun for a light by day, and the ordinances of the moon and of the stars for a light by night, Who stirreth up the sea, that the waves thereof roar, HaShem of hosts is His name: "If these ordinances depart from before Me," saith HaShem, "then the seed of Israel also shall cease from being a nation before Me for ever."

Thus saith HaShem: "If heaven above can be measured, and the foundations of the earth searched out beneath, then will I also cast off all the seed of Israel for all that they have done," saith HaShem.

Jewish History Did Not End At The Cross

Our Christian history cannot be changed, but I believe we can be. We will not be changed by some new doctrinal approach that can be packaged and then presented from the pulpits of America, but rather transformed by beginning to accept as absolute truth the promises God has established in the scriptures– *all* the

25

promises in the Bible, not just the ones made to the Christian church.

A current inaccuracy in segments of Christianity stems from the thinking that Jewish history ended at the cross of Christ. These believers are taught that the New Testament began at this moment in Jewish history, thus completing and annulling all the Old Testament's application.

As an evangelical Christian, a proponent of the Bible having been inspired by God, I believe that the God of Abraham, Isaac, and Jacob made numerous covenants with the Jewish people that He swore to be eternal.

I can hear some of my Christian friends protesting again, "JESUS– what about JESUS?"

What about Him?

I am a Christian Zionist, but I am not less of a Christian because I have become more of a Zionist. I still am persuaded that everyone, Jew and Gentile, needs the promised Messiah. I believe that Jesus is the Son of Man, the Son of David, the Son of God and Savior of the whole world. Because of my identification as a Christian, my Jewish readers already know that I believe this!

The problems in our relations with the Jewish people have absolutely nothing to do with Jesus: they stem from the tribulations we Christians have inflicted upon them for most of two millennia.

The contentious wall of separation between our communities is our fault, the result of our ancient and current Christian record of exceedingly arrogant, hypocritical, and wicked anti-Semitic actions toward the sons and daughters of Abraham, Isaac, and Jacob, "the apple of God's eye."

I pray this book illuminates for my Christian readers some graceful ways to give honest answers concerning the tenets of our faith. For my Jewish readers, I pray this book will be a source of growing hope for a future with trustworthy Zionist Christian friends.

The style and content of *Honest To God: The 10 Questions Jews Ask Christian Zionists* is not an intensely theological or exhaustive historic study guide, but rather a Christian primer for touching the apple of God's eye-- without poking it out!

Prologue

Intimate Collisions

My friend spent more than three decades as a teaching professor and president at one of America's highly regarded Christian seminaries. His name is listed as a noted scholar and contributor within the pages of numerous best-selling study Bibles. The professor knows exactly what he believes within the theology of the Hebrew and Greek Scriptures and has taught countless others these truths for well over fifty years.

He knew what he believed until the day his daughter tested his theology.

She had married young, and the marriage never took hold. Years of tears and counseling and immaturity had left this father's daughter a hollow shell of the effervescent woman he had kissed goodbye on her wedding day.

Her husband never hit her nor was he guilty of sexual infidelity. Rather, he was entirely unfaithful in following the commandments to nourish and cherish his wife. She had spiritually and emotionally died under his watch, and she could not find a way to continue with the non-relationship for another day.

Her father now warned her concerning the gravity of the steps she was considering.

D I V O R C E!

All caps and boldface with an exclamation point: this was exactly how his denomination looked upon the decision. Divorce was a heavy, dark, disturbing sin and those who succumbed to it were also bound to it for the rest of their natural days. Because his daughter's unfaithful husband had been faithful to his sexual vows, Dad-the-seminary-professor had to warn her that, should she end her marriage in divorce, she would never be able to marry again.

Isn't that a bit harsh, you ask?

Many evangelicals will answer cavalierly, "Talk to God. It's His Word, not mine!" Some Christians believe with all their hearts (as did my friend) that this is the definitive word and heart of our Creator concerning divorce and remarriage.

After many more tears and prayers, this young woman embarked upon the only path that left her any hope, divorcing the husband of her youth.

A number of years passed and the wounds of bewilderment, guilt and shame healed. This revitalized woman once again reflected the zest and joy of life she had known before her malnourished and ill-fated marriage. All was well in her heart and in her home.

And then she fell in love.

It happened at church, and to make things even more difficult, the honorable Christian fellow she fell in love with appeared to be the perfect companion her parents had hoped and prayed for since she was born.

How tragically too late was the arrival of this godly friend who would have loved, comforted, and cherished her until "death do they part."

An additional problem loomed, when her father began loving this man and imagining him as part of the family! A tsunami of conflict swelled within the heart of my theologically sound professor such as he had never experienced before. His convictions concerning divorce and remarriage were being tested for the first time in his life.

Until our theology collides with our life, it remains unproven dogma. It is often comprised of Biblical sound bites and interpretations we have compiled at a safe distance from personal cost for the belief. Much of the doctrine we adopt without testing is usually augmented by the influence of the religious community around us.

The father wept and prayed as he read the familiar words of Jesus.

Matthew, 19:8-9

Jesus said to them, "Moses, because of the hardness of your hearts, permitted you to divorce your wives, but from the beginning it was not so. And I say to you, whoever divorces his wife, except for sexual immorality, and marries another, commits adultery; and whoever marries her who is divorced commits adultery."

The professor recounted the many broken-hearted people he had instructed and imprisoned through the rigid adherence to the verse's apparent ironclad decree. It had been to some extent uncomplicated to force upon others what was now utterly unthinkable for his own flesh and blood

"How could God impose such an irrational life sentence upon my young, innocent daughter?" he questioned over and over again.

He could no more envision the unbearable prison of inconsistency causing his theological crisis than he could imagine his daughter without this gallant Christian man as her husband.

So he sought a way, and he found it through the testing of his theology. He went back to God and into the Bible he loved, frantically searching for truth like a father seeking after a lost child. In a nutshell, this was the Christian theological epiphany he experienced:

1) All sin is caused by human hardness of heart toward God.

2) As Christians, we believe that Jesus atones for and forgives all of our sins, as we ask Him to do so.

3) The failure of his daughter's first marriage was the result of sin. She needed to confess it as such, and she would then be cleansed of it (as with all sin we acknowledge.) Then the sin of divorce would be behind her and she would be free to marry again. Merciful God!

The professor just couldn't stop singing the chorus of the old Gospel spiritual:

O happy day! O happy day!
When Jesus washed all my sins away!

How could he have missed the mark for so many years concerning this controversial portion of scripture? How could he have been so callous and blinded in his righteousness when dealing with all the others who had tearfully sought his counsel concerning their marital failings?

How?
It was easy.

Until now, his theology had never collided with the yearnings of his heart. His doctrine regarding divorce had never been tested in the white-hot fire of real love.

End of story: His daughter married and lived very happily ever after. Professor-Grandpa considers his grandchildren and son-in-law amongst the richest blessings God has ever bestowed upon him. My professor friend, now in his mid-70s, continues to write and travel the nation, preaching and teaching.

I personally understand the horrifying and long-lasting consequences divorce can inflict upon families and children. My simplification of this one story should not be taken as a suggestion to follow its example to escape the common trials of marriage. For the Christian reader who adheres to the "no-remarriage" doctrine of divorce, I suggest you have not yet been tested in this area of your faith. If you associate with a Christian you believe is living in the continued state of adultery by remarrying after a divorce for any cause other than infidelity, then you are sinning by disobeying the following Scripture.

I Corinthians 5:1
But now I am writing you that you must not associate with anyone who calls himself a brother but is sexually immora...

Every church has members who have remarried after failed marriages. Some of these men and women have gone through a divorce that was due not to infidelity, but rather to other insurmountable problems within the marriage. These "adulterous" Christians take Communion with you, they teach in your Sunday Schools, and they worship with you every Sunday.

The fact that you and your leaders do not root them out and remove them from your midst until they cease their "immoral" lifestyle makes you as guilty of sin as you believe they are.

What about these marriages that have now produced children? How do you approach and associate with these families and remain true to your interpretation of what Jesus was saying in Matthew 19:8-9? The fact is, you probably don't, but neither do you address the biblical problem this creates within your own theology and life.

My point: It is easy to say we believe something until we are forced to live out our untested theology-- when it intimately touches our own lives.

In the writings of Samuel 2:12, we find King David about to have his theology tested in a very personal and life-altering way. In the midst of a normal day, while listening to the concerns of his subjects, King David heard a story so horrendously unjust that it filled him with absolute fury.

> *There were two men in the same city – one rich, the other poor. The rich man had huge flocks of sheep, herds of cattle. The poor man had nothing but one little female lamb, which he had bought and raised. It grew up with him and his children as a member of the family. It ate off his plate and drank from his cup and slept on his bed. It was like a daughter to him. One day a traveler dropped in on the rich man.*

> *He was too stingy to take an animal from his own herds or flocks to make a meal for his visitor, so he took the poor man's lamb and prepared a meal to set before his guest.*

There was no need for David to summon his counselors or seek the Almighty in prayer. Unable to contain himself, he shouted out an immediate and righteous judgment in response to the act of savagery that had been committed under his watch.

> *"As surely as the Lord lives," he vowed, "any man who would do such a thing deserves to die! He must first repay*

four lambs to the poor man for the one he stole and for having no pity!"

The man commissioned by the Almighty to bring this matter before King David endured his response, and then answered him-- with the rest of the story:

Then Nathan the prophet said to David, "You are that man! The Lord, the God of Israel, says: 'I anointed you king of Israel and saved you from the power of Saul. I gave you your master's house and his wives and the kingdoms of Israel and Judah. And if that had not been enough, I would have given you much, much more. Why, then, have you despised the word of The Lord and done this horrible deed? For you have murdered Uriah the Hittite with the sword of the Ammonites and stolen his wife. From this time on, your family will live by the sword because you have despised me by taking Uriah's wife to be your own.

'Because of what you have done, I will cause your own household to rebel against you. I will give your wives to another man before your very eyes, and he will go to bed with them in public view. You did it secretly, but I will make this happen to you openly in the sight of all Israel.'"

"Gulp," David silently responded. The king immediately had a change of heart in the matter and humbly replied, "I have sinned against The Lord." King David's theology concerning the judgments, righteousness, and the mercy of God just had an intimate collision with his life.

We can see the effects this encounter had on his understanding of the God of Israel by reading Psalm 51 and other songs of praise he wrote in the days that followed this tragic chapter of his life.

Psalm 51:1

Have mercy on me, O God, because of your unfailing love – because of your great compassion blot out the stain of my sins.

I present these stories to my readers because of the great and urgent need for individual, personal reflection by Christians – a self-examination of the authenticity of our love and support for the Jewish people.

I suggest that until our Zionist theology interrupts our lives through intimate collisions with our hearts, it remains untested and adolescent in nature.

Thousands upon thousands of Christian Zionists stand with Israel because it is written in the Bible to do so. They "love" the Jewish people because they know they should –and this is good. But you cannot genuinely love what you do not intimately know, nor can you effectively support someone from an emotional distance. Sadly, many Christian Zionists do not have one close Jewish friend. Absent such relationships, these Christians never eat at Jewish homes, attend Jewish children's birthday parties or bar mitzvahs/bat mitzvahs, or weep in prayer over personal trials afflicting Jewish families. These same Christian supporters of Israel have never received the blessing of a rabbi's prayer for them; nor have they heard, felt or understood the real fears and hopes of the Jewish people.

Partially due to the Christian distance from Jewish friendships, we remain abstractly theological, emotionally detached from the Jewish people. These chasms often result in causing Jews to feel that they are nothing more than our conversion targets or our self-interested good-luck charms (per Genesis 12:3: *I will bless those who bless you.*)

My journey as a Christian Zionist has awakened me to these ominous relational chasms, as you will see recounted through numerous stories in this book. Please read with patience the apparent detours these personal experiences take, as they are each essential to understanding my responses to these *10 Questions Jews Ask Christian Zionists.*

I pray this book will touch your life and theology, as well as encourage you to watch for your own paths of intimate encounters as you stand with God's chosen people-- the descendants of Abraham, Isaac and Jacob.

Question 1

"Does the Christian community have the patience for us?"

Standard Christian Answer:
"I have no idea what your question means."

I received a call from The Israel/Christian Nexus and was invited to participate in an event titled "Honest to God: A Candid Conversation between a Rabbi and a Pastor."

> *For My Christian Readers:*
> The Israel-Christian Nexus was created in 2002 to bring Christians and Jews together in support of the people and state of Israel. Established by one of Israel's founding fathers and one of its most decorated war heroes, General (retired) Shimon Erem, the mission of the Israel-Christian Nexus is to strengthen the alliance between Jews and Christians in defense of our shared Judeo-Christian values and to educate and mobilize the two communities for sustained action in solidarity with the nation and people of Israel. (General Erem of blessed memory died on May 27, 2012)

The rabbi and I did not rehearse the questions ahead of time, nor did we put any boundaries on the topics that would be discussed. Together we hoped that our interaction would embody exactly what the title had promised. As the workshop progressed, it grew frighteningly intimate as we tearfully exhausted each other and the allotted time for our presentation.

The rabbi pondered out loud one last question I could tell was of enormous significance to him.

"Pastor?" he cautiously inquired, both dreading and hoping in the answer he might hear, "Does the Christian community have the patience for us?"

Scanning my cerebral hard disk for any sort of information on how to answer such a troubling concern, I bought myself some time by quipping, "Patience? My wife and I have raised teenagers–you guys are easy!"

Getting Past "Dialogue"

While I was spending time with a new pastor in town, he and I began talking about the work of Christian Zionists. My heart quickens and my eyes begin to shine whenever I am turned loose on the subject of Christians and Jews. As I spoke of my deep and brotherly love for my Jewish friends, the pastor leaned back in his chair and, wrinkling his forehead, asked, "So what is the dialogue like when you are speaking with Jews?"

"Dialogue?"

Now that is an incredibly safe, sterile, and strained vocabulary to describe a love relationship.

I don't have "dialogue" with my children. I certainly don't have dialogue within the intimacies of my marriage, and I don't have dialogue when speaking with Jews.

When my Jewish friends and I have fellowship, we do so face to face, as equals, as brothers and sisters. And why not? We are the only two faith communities on earth that recognize the God of Abraham, Isaac and Jacob as our heavenly Abba.

For My Christian Readers:
The children of my Jewish friends call their fathers Abba, as do the children of my Suni Muslim neighbors. Though I have a loving

relationship with my Muslim neighbors, I purposely omit them as believers in the God of our Hebrew and New Testament Bible. They are not.

At this point, a number of Christian readers are saying, "Well, I can only have true fellowship with other Christians."

Yea, our history has shown that we think and live that way.

I'm not talking about the "fellowship" of something like interfaith marriages here. Both the Torah and New Testament discourage those unions and I won't perform them. Neither am I referring to the "fellowship" or communion of our faith. As Christians, we see some faith issues differently than the Torah-loving Jewish community. We therefore practice portions of our faith in different ways that may not be transferable into some aspects of our fellowship with each other.

But I do have fellowship with my Jewish friends over the many truths of God we see as one: many of these truths taught to us by the faithfulness of the Jews!

We have deep fellowship concerning our love, hopes and fears concerning our children and our marriages.

I have often had hilarious and pain-filled fellowship with Jewish leaders concerning the tendencies in both our flocks for the sheep to gnaw on their shepherds rather than feast on the Word of God.

Many of my Jewish friends accompany me when I'm ministering in their cities, and my wife and I often attend their synagogue services as well.

Call it what you will, I experience many times of rich fellowship with my Jewish buddies. And no matter what you call it, until we as Christians establish a true bond of love within all of our personal relationships, we are sorely missing the mark set by our Chief Rabbi.

For My Christian Readers:
Remembering that Jesus was repeatedly criticized for having "fellowship" with folks outside of his faith community, please re-evaluate the boundaries you have placed around your life when it comes to creating loving relationships with those who are not members of your church association. Sadly, many Christians have very few if any meaningful relationships other than those within the local church they attend.

So…"dialogue"?

Let's leave dialogue for politicians and diplomats.

"Honest to God… A Candid Conversation between a Rabbi and a Pastor," had rocketed way past dialogue as the spirit of God fell upon all of us in the room. Each interaction we shared was drenched with healing tears of hope that appeared to be airborne as our weeping contagiously spread throughout the entire sanctuary. (At one point my wife actually flung a box of tissues on the stage so the rabbi and I could blow our noses and put an end to our increasingly irritating, unprofessional, and amplified sniffling into the lapel microphones we were wearing.)

Rabbi Isaac faintly smiled and asked again, "Does the Christian community have the patience for us?"

Why would a rabbi, who had been given a free pass on examining the theology and thoughts of a Christian Zionist pastor, ask such a question?

As I prayed for understanding, I began to recollect the history of the Jewish people in Christian societies—a history of relentless persecution that cried out for an answer.

Awareness of this Christian/Jewish record is absolutely essential for an elementary understanding of the rational hesitancy of the Jewish community to fully embrace our new proclaimed love for them. It may also begin to help each of us in trying to understand the mysterious question my rabbi friend asked in such a gracious manner.

"The Jews are a nervous people. Nineteen centuries of Christian love have taken a toll." Benjamin Disraeli (1804-1881), England's only Jewish Prime Minister.

Persecution of Jews by Christians

Please, take the time to reflect upon Christianity's horrid historic testimony and the personal stories of those who were the recipients of our wicked transgressions. As you do, try to grasp the cumulative heartbreaking wounds this has left upon the Jewish people.

A.D. 170: Notable early Christian apologist Tertullain taught that the Jews were "the Cains, the murderers, and were rejected as the Chosen People of God." (*Adversus Judaeos.*)

220: Origen, one of the most distinguished of the early fathers of the Christian Church, declared the Jews as dangerous enemies of Christians.

306: The church Synod of Elvira banned marriages, sexual intercourse and community contacts between Christians and Jews.

315: Constantine published the Edict of Milan, which extended religious tolerance to Christians. Jews lost many rights with this edict. They were no longer permitted to live in Jerusalem or to proselytize.

325: The Council of Nicea decided to separate the celebration of Easter from the Jewish Passover. They stated: "For it is unbecoming beyond measure that on this holiest of festivals we should follow the customs of the Jews. Henceforth let us have nothing in common with this odious people ... We ought not, therefore, to have anything in common with the Jews ... Our worship follows a more convenient course. We desire, dearest brethren, to separate ourselves from the detestable company of the Jews. How, then, could we follow these Jews, who are almost certainly blinded."

337: Christian Emperor Constantius created a law that made the marriage of a Jewish man to a Christian punishable by death.

339: Converting to Judaism became a criminal offense.

343-381: The Laodicean Synod approved Canon 38: "It is not lawful [for Christians] to receive unleavened bread from the Jews, nor to be partakers of their impiety."

367-376: St. Hilary of Poitiers referred to Jews as a perverse people whom God has cursed forever. St. Ephroem referred to synagogues as brothels.

379-395: Emperor Theodosius the Great permitted the destruction of synagogues if it served a religious purpose. Christianity became the state religion of the Roman Empire at this time.

380: The bishop of Milan was responsible for the burning of a synagogue; he referred to it as "an act pleasing to God." St. Ambrose called the synagogue "a place of unbelief, a home of impiety, a refuge of insanity, damned by God Himself."

400: Calling the synagogue a "brothel and theater" and "a cave of pirates and the lair of wild beasts," St. John Chrysostom wrote that "the Jews behave no better than hogs and goats in their lewd grossness and the excesses of their gluttony."

415: The Bishop of Alexandria, St. Cyril, expelled the Jews from that Egyptian city.

415: St. Augustine wrote "The true image of the Hebrew is Judas Iscariot, who sells the Lord for silver. The Jew can never understand the Scriptures and forever will bear the guilt for the death of Jesus."

418: St. Jerome, who created the Vulgate translation of the Bible, wrote of a synagogue: "If you call it a brothel, a den of vice, the Devil's refuge, Satan's fortress, a place to deprave the soul, an abyss of every conceivable disaster or whatever you will, you are still saying less than it deserves."

489-519: Christian mobs destroyed the synagogues in Antioch, Daphne (near Antioch) and Ravenna.

528: Emperor Justinian (527-564) passed the Justinian Code. It prohibited Jews from building synagogues, reading the Bible in Hebrew, assembling in public, celebrating Passover before Easter, and testifying against Christians in court.

535: The Synod of Claremont decreed that Jews could not hold public office or have authority over Christians.

538: The Third and Fourth Councils of Orléans prohibited Jews from appearing in public during the Easter season. Canon 30 decreed: "From the Thursday before Easter for four days, Jews may not appear in the company of Christians." Marriages between Christians and Jews were prohibited. Christians were prohibited from converting to Judaism.

561: The bishop of Uzes expelled Jews from his diocese in France.

591: Pope St. Gregory the Great decreed that Jews were not to be forced into baptism "lest they return to their former superstition and die the worse for having been born again."

612: Jews were not allowed to own land, to be farmers or enter certain trades.

613: Serious persecution began in Spain. Jews were given the options of either leaving Spain or converting to Christianity. Jewish children over six years of age were taken from their parents and given a Christian education.

692: Canon II of the Quinisext Council stated: "Let no one in the priestly order nor any layman eat the unleavened bread of t he Jews, nor have any familiar intercourse with them, nor summon them in illness, nor receive medicines from them, nor bathe with them; but if anyone shall take in hand to do so, if he is a cleric, let him be deposed, but if a layman, let him be cut off."

694: The 17th Church Council of Toledo, Spain defined Jews as the serfs of the prince. This was based, in part, on the beliefs by Chrysostom, Origen, Jerome and other Church fathers that God punished the Jews with perpetual slavery because of their responsibility for the execution of Jesus.

722: Leo III outlawed Judaism. Jews were baptized against their will.

830: Agobard, Archbishop of Lyons, wrote anti-Jewish pamphlets in which he referred to Jews as "sons of darkness."

855: Jews were exiled from Italy.

937: Pope Leo VII encouraged his newly appointed archbishop of Mainz to expel all Jews who refused to be baptized.

1010: In Rouen, Orléans, Limoges, Mainz, and Rome, Jews were converted by force, massacred, or expelled.

1050: The Synod of Narbonne prohibited Christians from living in the homes of Jews.

1078: Pope Gregory VII decreed: "Jews could not hold office or be superiors to Christians."

1078: The Synod of Gerona forced Jews to pay church taxes.

1081: Pope Gregory VII wrote to King Alphonso of Spain, telling him that if he allowed Jews to be lords over Christians, he would be oppressing the Church and exalting "the Synagogue of Satan."

Crusaders

"In an unheard-of and unprecedented outburst of cruelty, they [crusaders] have slaughtered, in this mad hostility, two thousand and five hundred of them; old and young as well as pregnant women. Some were mortally wounded and others trampled like mud under the feet of horses. They burned their books and, for greater shame and disgrace, they exposed the bodies of those thus killed for food to the birds of heaven and their flesh to the beasts of the earth. After hideously and shamefully treating those who remained alive after this massacre, they carried off their goods and consumed them. And in order that they may be able to hide such an inhuman crime under the cover of virtue, and in some way justify their unholy cause, they represent themselves as having done the above and threaten to do worse, on the ground that they (the Jews) refuse to be baptized."
(Pope Gregory IX, in a letter to the French kings, September 1236)

1096: The First Crusade was launched. Although the prime goal of the crusades was to liberate Jerusalem from the Muslims, Jews were a secondary target. As the soldiers passed

45

through Europe on the way to the Holy Land, large numbers of Jews were challenged: "Christ-killers, embrace the Cross or die!" Twelve thousand Jews in the Rhine Valley alone were killed in the first Crusade.

This behavior continued for eight additional crusades until the ninth in 1272. The Jewish chronicler reported: "The enemies stripped them naked and dragged them off, granting quarter to none, save those few who accepted baptism. The number of the slain was eight hundred in these two days." The chronicler Guibert de Nogent reported that the Rouen Crusaders said: "We desire to go and fight God's enemies in the East; but we have before our eyes certain Jews, a race more unfavorable to God than any other."

1099: The Crusaders forced all the Jews of Jerusalem into a central synagogue and set it on fire. Those who tried to escape were forced back into the burning building.

1121: Jews were exiled from Flanders (part of present-day Belgium).

1130: Some Jews in London allegedly killed a sick man. The Jewish people in the city were required to pay one million marks as compensation.

1146: The Second Crusade began. A French Monk, Rudolf, called for the destruction of the Jews.

1179: Canon 24 of the Third Lateran Council stated: "Jews should be slaves to Christians and at the same time be treated kindly due of humanitarian considerations." Canon 26 stated: "The testimony of Christians against Jews is to be preferred in all causes where they use their own witnesses against Christians."

1180: King Philip Augustus of France arbitrarily seized all Jewish property and expelled the Jews from the country. The Jews were allowed to sell all movable possessions, but their land and houses were stolen by the king.

1189: Jews were persecuted in England. The Crown claimed all Jewish possessions. Most of their houses were burned.

1190: The Third Crusade, led by Richard the Lion-Hearted, stirred anti-Jewish fervor that resulted in the mass suicide of the York Jews in Clifford's Tower on March 16.

1205: Pope Innocent III wrote to the archbishops of Sens and Paris that "the Jews, by their own guilt, are consigned to perpetual servitude because they crucified the Lord...As slaves rejected by God, in whose death they wickedly conspire, they shall by the effect of this very action, recognize themselves as the slaves of those whom Christ's death set free..."

1215: The Fourth Lateran Council approved canon laws requiring that "Jews and Muslims shall wear a special dress," which included a badge in the form of a ring. This was to enable them to be easily distinguished from Christians. This practice later spread to other countries.

1227: The Synod of Narbonne required Jews to wear an oval badge. This requirement would be reinstated during the 1930's by Adolf Hitler, who replaced the oval with the Star of David.

1229: The Spanish Inquisition started. Later, in 1252, Pope Innocent IV authorized the use of torture by the Inquisitors.

1235: Thirty-four Jews were burned to death in Fulda, Germany, on a blood-libel charge.

Blood Libel

In 1144 AD, an unfounded rumor began in eastern England that Jews had kidnapped a Christian child, tied him to a cross, stabbed his head to simulate Jesus' crown of thorns, killed him, drained his body completely of blood, and mixed the blood into matzos (unleavened bread) at the time of Passover.

The rumor was started by a Jew, Theobald, who had become a Christian monk. He said that Jewish representatives gathered each year in Narbonne, France and decided in which city a Christian child would be sacrificed. The boy involved in the 1144 hoax became known as St. William of Norwich. Many people made pilgrimages to his tomb and claimed that miracles had resulted from appeals to St. William.

The myth shows a complete lack of understanding of mainline Judaism. Aside from the prohibition of killing innocent persons, the Torah specifically forbids the eating or drinking of any form of blood in any quantity. However, reality never has had much of an impact on blood libel myths. These rumors lasted for many centuries; even today they have not completely disappeared.

Pope Innocent IV ordered a study in 1247 CE. His investigators found that the myth was a Christian invention used to justify persecution of the Jews. At least four other popes subsequently vindicated the Jews. However, the accusations, trials, and executions continued. In 1817, Czar Alexander I of Russia declared that the blood libel was a myth. Even that announcement did not stop the accusations against Jews in that country.
Holy shrines were erected to honor innocent Christian victims, and well into the twentieth century churches throughout Europe displayed knives and other instruments that Jews purportedly used for these rituals.

Caricatures of hunchbacked Jews with horns and fangs were depicted in works of art and carved as decoration into stone bridges. Proclaimed by parish priests to be the gospel truth, each recurrence of the blood libel charge added to its credence, prompting yet more accusations. This vicious cycle continued to spiral."

1236: Pope Gregory ordered that church leaders in England, France, Portugal and Spain confiscated Jewish books on the first Saturday of Lent.

1259: A synod of the archdiocese in Mainz ordered Jews to wear yellow badges.

1261: Duke Henry III of Brabant, Belgium, stated in his will that "Jews... must be expelled from Brabant and totally annihilated so that not a single one remains, except those who are willing to trade, like all other tradesmen, without money-lending and usury."

1267: The Synod of Vienna ordered Jews to wear horned hats. Thomas Aquinas said that Jews should live in perpetual servitude. The Synod of Breslau decreed compulsory ghettos for Jews.

1279: The Synod of Ofen decreed that Christians could not sell or rent real estate to Jews.

1290: Jews were exiled from England and southern Italy.

1294: Jews were expelled from Bern.

1298: Jews were persecuted in Austria, Bavaria and Franconia. 140 Jewish communities were destroyed; more than 100,000 Jews were killed over a six-month period.

1298: The Jews of Röttingen were charged with profaning the Host. Rindfleisch, a nobleman of that place, pretending to have received a mission from heaven to avenge this desecration and to exterminate "the accursed race of the

Jews," gathered a mob and burned the Jews of Röttingen at the stake. Under his leadership the mob went from town to town, killing all the Jews who fell into their power, save those who accepted Christianity. The great community of Würzburgwas annihilated.

Profaning the Host

"Jews were frequently accused of desecrating the Host (Communion bread or wafer), an accusation equal in gravity in the Catholic theology of those days to that of desecrating relics and images of Jesus and the Saints. The Jews were alleged to steal the host or to acquire it by purchase or bribery, to break it or boil it or to stick needles into it, thus causing it to bleed. Even when such an accusation was supported only by the testimony of a thief, a recent convert, or someone having a grudge against the accused Jews, the alleged perpetrators were put on trial and–on evidence that was often preposterous, or after a confession exacted by torture–were condemned and burned, sometimes with all the other Jews of the place."

1306: 100,000 Jews were exiled from France. They left with only the clothes on their backs, and food for only one day.

1320: 40,000 French shepherds went to Palestine on the Shepherd Crusade. On the way, 140 Jewish communities were destroyed. "The shepherds laid siege to all the Jews who had come from all sides to take refuge... the Jews defended themselves heroically...but their resistance served no purpose, for the shepherds slaughtered a great number of the besieged Jews by smoke and by fire....

The Jews, realizing that they would not escape alive, preferred to kill themselves... They chose one of their number (and) this man put some five hundred of them to death, with their consent. He then descended from the castle tower with the few Jewish children who still remained alive....

They killed him by quartering. They spared the children, whom they made Catholics by baptism."

1321: In Guienne, France, Jews were accused of having incited criminals to poison wells. 5,000 Jews were burned alive at the stake.

1338: The councilors of Freiburg banned the performance of anti-Jewish scenes from the town's passion play because of the lethal bloody reactions against Jews that had followed such performances.

1347: The Black Death, bubonic plague, originated in the Far East.

The Black Death

"In the year 1348 that terrible contagion known as the Black Death, which journeyed from the East to devastate the whole of Europe, appeared at Strasbourg. Everywhere famine, floods, the inversion of the seasons, strange appearances in the sky, had been its precursors. In the Mediterranean Sea, as afterwards in the Baltic, ships were discovered drifting masterless, filled only by plague-stricken corpses. Every man dreaded, not merely the touch and the breath of his neighbor, but his very gaze, so subtle and so swift seemed the infection.

In many parts of France it was computed that only two out of every twenty inhabitants were left alive. In Strasbourg sixteen thousand perished; in Avignon sixty thousand. In Paris, at one time, four or five hundred were dying in a day.

In a frenzy of terror and revenge the people fell upon the miserable Jews. They were accused of poisoning the wells, and every heart was steeled against them. Fear seemed to render all classes more ferocious, and the man who might sicken and die tomorrow found a wretched compensation in inflicting death today on the imagined authors of his danger.

Toledo was supposed to be the center of an atrocious scheme by which the Jews, some after torture and some in terror of it, confessed that they had received poison for that purpose. Bishops, nobles and chief citizens held a diet at Binnefeld in Alsace, to concert measures of persecution. The deputies of Strasbourg, to their honor be it spoken, declared that nothing had been proved against the Jews. Their bishop was the most pitiless advocate of massacre. The result was a league of priests, lords, and people, to slay or banish every Jew. Some Christians, who had sought from pity or from avarice to save them, perished in the same flames. No power could stem the torrent.

The people had tasted blood; the priest had no mercy for the murderers of the Lord; the baron had debts easily discharged by the death of his creditor. At Strasbourg a monster scaffold was erected in the Jewish burial ground, and two thousand were burnt alive. At Basle all the Jews were burnt together in a wooden edifice erected for the purpose. At Spires they set their quarter in flames and perished by their own hands. A guard kept out the populace while men commissioned by the senate hunted for treasure among the smoking ruins. The corrupting bodies of those slain in the streets were put in empty wine casks and rolled into the Rhine. When the rage for slaughter had subsided, hands, red with Hebrew blood were piously employed in building belfries and repairing churches with Jewish tombstones and the materials of Jewish houses."

As people looked around for someone to blame for the pestilence, they noted that a smaller percentage of Jews than Christians caught the disease. (This was undoubtedly due to Jewish sanitary and kosher dietary laws.) Rumors circulated that Satan was protecting the Jews. The solution was to torture, murder and burn the Jews.

In Bavaria 12,000 Jews perished; in the small town of Erfurt, 3,000; in Rue Brulée, 2,000 Jews; near Tours an immense trench was dug, filled with blazing wood, and in a single day 160 Jews were burned. In Strasberg 2,000 Jews were burned. In Maintz 6,000 were killed; in Worms, 400.

1350: Jews were expelled from many parts of Germany.

1354: 12,000 Jews were executed in Toledo, Spain.

1367: Jews were expelled from Hungary.

1374: "An epidemic of possession broke out in the lower Rhine region of what is now Germany. People were seen "dancing, jumping and [engaging in] wild raving." This was triggered by enthusiastic revels on St. John's Day, a Christianized version of an ancient pagan seasonal celebration that was still observed by the populace. The epidemic spread throughout the Rhine and much of the Netherlands and Germany. Crowds of 500 or more dancers would be overcome together. Exorcisms were tried and pilgrimages were made to the shrine of St. Vitus without success. A rumor spread that God was angry because Christians had been excessively tolerant towards the Jews; God had cursed Europe as He did King Saul when he showed mercy towards God's enemies in the Old Testament. Jews were plundered, tortured and murdered by tens of thousands. The epidemic finally faded away two centuries later, in the late 16th century."

1381: Jews were expelled from Strasbourg.

1391: Jewish persecutions began in Seville and in 70 other Jewish communities throughout Spain.

1394: For the second time, Jews were expelled from France.

1420: Jews were expelled from Mainz by the archbishop.

1421: Jews were expelled from Austria.

1424: Jews were expelled from Fribourg and Zurich.

1426: Jews were expelled from Cologne.

1432: Jews were expelled from Saxony.

1431: The Council of Basel forbade Jews to go to universities, prohibited them from acting as agents in the conclusion of contracts between Christians, and required that they attend church sermons.

1434: Jewish men in Augsburg had to sew yellow buttons to their clothes. Across Europe, Jews were forced to wear a long undergarment, an overcoat with a yellow patch, bells and t all pointed yellow hats with a large button on them.

1453: The Franciscan monk Capistrano persuaded the King of Poland to terminate all Jewish civil rights.

1492: Jews were given the choice of being baptized as Christians or banished from Spain. 300,000 left Spain, penniless. Many migrated to Turkey, where they found tolerance among the Muslims. Others converted to Christianity but often continued to practice Judaism in secret.

1497: Jews were banished from Portugal. 20,000 left the country rather than be baptized.

1516: The Governor of the Republic of Venice decided that Jews would be permitted to live in only one area of the city. It was located in the South Girolamo parish and was called the "Ghetto Novo." This was the first ghetto in Europe. Hitler would make use of the concept in the 1930s.

1523: Martin Luther distributed his essay "That Jesus Was Born a Jew." At this time, he hoped that large numbers of Jews would convert to Christianity.

"That Jesus Was Born a Jew" Martin Luther (1523)

"If I had been a Jew and had seen such dolts and blockheads govern and teach the Christian faith, I would sooner have become a hog than a Christian. They have dealt with the Jews as if they were dogs rather than human beings; they have done little else than deride them and seize their property.

"When they baptize them they show them nothing of Christian doctrine or life, but only subject them to popishness and monkery. If the apostles, who also were Jews, had dealt with us Gentiles as we Gentiles deal with the Jews, there would never have been a Christian among the Gentiles. When we are inclined to boast of our position [as Christians] we should remember that we are but Gentiles, while the Jews are of the lineage of Christ. We are aliens and in-laws; they are blood relatives, cousins, and brothers of our Lord. Therefore, if one is to boast of flesh and blood the Jews are actually nearer to Christ than we are.

"If we really want to help them, we must be guided in our dealings with them not by papal law but by the law of Christian love. We must receive them cordially, and permit them to trade and work with us, that they may have occasion and opportunity to associate with us, hear our Christian teaching, and witness our Christian life. If some of them should prove stiff-necked, what of it? After all, we ourselves are not all good Christians either."

1540: Jews were exiled from Naples.

1543: Now distressed by the reluctance of Jews to convert to Christianity, Martin Luther developed a hatred for Jews, as expressed in his 65,000-word treatise "On the Jews and Their Lies."

"On the Jews and Their Lies" Martin Luther (1543)

"I have come to the conclusion that the Jews will always curse and blaspheme God and his King Christ, as all the prophets have predicted.... For they are thus given over by the wrath of God to reprobation, that they may become incorrigible, as Ecclesiastes says, for every one who is incorrigible is rendered worse rather than better by correction.

"...(E)ject them forever from this country. For, as we have heard, God's anger with them is so intense that gentle mercy will only tend to make them worse and worse, while sharp mercy will reform them but little. Therefore, in any case, away with them! What then shall we Christians do with this damned, rejected race of Jews?

"First, their synagogues or churches should be set on fire....

"Secondly, their homes should likewise be broken down and destroyed.... They ought to be put under one roof or in a stable, like Gypsies.

"Thirdly, they should be deprived of their prayer books and Talmuds in which such idolatry, lies, cursing and blasphemy are taught.

"Fourthly, their rabbis must be forbidden under threat of death to teach any more....

"Fifthly, passport and traveling privileges should be absolutely forbidden to the Jews....

"Sixthly, they ought to be stopped from usury. All their cash and valuables of silver and gold ought to be taken from them and put aside for safe keeping...

"Seventhly, let the young and strong Jews and Jewesses be given the flail, the axe, the hoe, the spade, the distaff, and spindle and let them earn their bread by the sweat of their noses as in enjoined upon Adam's children....

"To sum up, dear princes and nobles who have Jews in your domains, if this advice of mine does not suit you, then find a better one so that you and we may all be free of this insufferable devilish burden – the Jews."

It was not until 1994 that the Lutheran Church publicly responded and repented of these abominable writings of their founder. In their "Declaration of the Evangelical Lutheran Church in America to the Jewish Community" (April 18, 1994), they conceded "Luther's anti-Judaic diatribes" and expressed "deep and abiding sorrow over their tragic effects on subsequent generations."

"The power of life and death are in the tongue" (Proverbs 18:21) and the seeds of Luther's deadly words lay fallow throughout all of Europe, until history brought a grim reaper to water and harvest the crop they produced. In Mein Kampf, Adolph Hitler commended Luther as ". . . a great warrior, a true statesman, and a great reformer."

What did the Protestant reformer and Hitler have in common? Their hatred of the Jewish people.

1550: Jews were exiled from Genoa and Venice.

1555: *Cum nimis absurdum*, a Roman Catholic Papal bull (official letter of decree from the Pope) required Jews to wear badges and live in ghettos. They were not allowed to own property outside the ghetto. Living conditions were dreadful: over 3,000 people were forced to live on about eight acres of land. Women had to wear yellow veils or scarfs; men had to wear a piece of yellow cloth on their hats.

1582: Jews were expelled from Holland.

1648: Bogdan Chmielnicki led an uprising against Polish rule in the Ukraine. The secondary goal of Chmielnicki and his followers was to exterminate all Jews in the country. The massacre began with the slaughter of about 6,000 Jews in Nemirov. Other major mass murders occurred in Tulchin, Polonnoye, Volhynia, Bar, Lvov, etc. Jewish records estimate that a total of 100,000 Jews were murdered and 300 communities destroyed. (Unbelievably, Chmielnicki is considered a nationalist hero in the Ukraine. In Kiev there is a large statue in the main square erected in his honor.)

Slaughter of the Jews in Russia

"On the same day 1,500 people were killed in the city of Human in Russia on the Sabbath. The nobles [Cossacks] with whom the wicked mob had again made an alliance chased all the Jews from the city into the fields and vineyards where the villains surrounded them in a circle, stripped them to their skin and ordered them to lie on the ground.

"The villains spoke to the Jews with friendly and consoling words: 'Why do you want to be killed, strangled and slaughtered like an offering to your God who poured out His anger upon you without mercy? Would it not be safer for you to worship our gods, our images and crosses and we would form one people which would unite together?'

"But the holy and faithful people who so often allowed themselves to be murdered for the sake of the Lord, raised their voices together to the Almighty in Heaven and cried: 'Hear, O Israel the Lord our God, the Holy One and the King of the Universe, we have been murdered for Thy sake so often already. O, Lord God of Israel let us remain faithful to Thee.' Now the villains turned upon them and there was not one of them who did not fall victim."

1794: Jewish men were forced to serve twenty-five years in the Russian military. Hundreds of thousands of Jews were forced to leave their homes in Russia.

1806: A French Jesuit Priest, Abbe Barruel, wrote a treatise blaming the Masonic Order for the French Revolution. He later issued a letter alleging that Jews, not the Masons, were the guilty party. This triggered a belief in an international Jewish conspiracy in Germany, Poland and some other European countries later in the 19th century.

1819: During the late 18th and early 19th centuries, many European Jews lobbied their governments for emancipation. They sought citizenship as well as the same rights and treatment enjoyed by non-Jews. This appears to have provoked anti-Semites to engage in sporadic anti-Jewish violence. Jews and their property were attacked first in Wuerzburg, Germany, in 1819; the rioting spread across Germany and eventually reached as far as Denmark and Poland.

1840: A rumor spread in Syria that some Jews were responsible for the ritual killing of a Roman Catholic monk and his servant. As a result of horrendous treatment, some local Jews confessed to a crime they did not commit.

1846-1878: Pope Pius IX restored all the previous restrictions against the Jews within the Vatican state. All Jews under Papal control were confined to Rome's ghetto, the last one in Europe until the Nazi era restored the church's practice. On September 3, 2000, Pope John Paul II would beatify Pius IX, granting the last step before sainthood. He explained: "Beatifying a son of the church does not celebrate particular historic choices that he has made, but rather points him out for imitation and for veneration for his virtue."

1858: Edgardo Mortara, six years old, was kidnapped from his Jewish family by Roman Catholic officials after they found out that a maid had secretly baptized him. He was not returned to his family but was raised a Catholic. He eventually became a priest.

1881: Alexander II of Russia was assassinated by radicals. The Jews were blamed. About 200 individual pogroms against the Jews followed. Thousands of Jews became homeless and impoverished.

Pogroms

A *pogrom* is an organized and often officially encouraged persecution or massacre of a minority group, especially one conducted against the Jews. In Russia, a pogrom was typically a mob riot against Jewish individuals, shops, homes or businesses.

"The term pogrom became commonly used in English after a large-scale wave of anti-Jewish riots swept through southwestern Imperial Russia in 1881-1884. A much bloodier wave of pogroms broke out in 1903-1906, leaving an estimated 2,000 Jews dead and many more wounded, as the Jews took to arms to defend their families and property from the attackers.

"Many pogroms accompanied the Revolution of 1917, and in the ensuing Russian Civil War, an estimated 70,000 to 250,000 civilian Jews were killed in the atrocities throughout the former Russian Empire; the number of Jewish orphans exceeded 300,000. Even after the end of World War II, there were still a few pogroms in Poland, such as the Kraków pogrom on August 11, 1945 or the infamous Kielce pogrom of 1946."

1893: Anti-Semitic parties won sixteen seats in the German Reichstag.

1894: Captain Alfred Dreyfus, an officer of Jewish background on the French general staff, was convicted of treason. The evidence against him consisted of a piece of paper from his wastebasket in another person's handwriting, and papers forged by anti-Semitic officers. He received a life sentence on Devil's Island, off the coast of South America.

The French government was aware that a Major Esterhazy was actually guilty. The church, government and army united to suppress the truth. Writer Emile Zola and politician Jean Jaurès fought for justice and human rights. After ten years, the French government fell and Dreyfus was declared totally innocent.

"The Dreyfus Affair" was worldwide news for years. It motivated journalist Theodor Herzl to write a book in 1896 entitled *The Jewish State: A Modern Solution to the Jewish Question*. This book led to the founding of the Zionist movement that fought for a Jewish Homeland. A half-century later, the state of Israel would be born.

1903: At Easter, government agents organized an anti-Jewish pogrom in Kishinev, Moldova, Russia. The local newspaper published a series of inflammatory articles. A Christian child was discovered murdered and a young

Christian woman at the Jewish Hospital committed suicide. Jews were blamed for the deaths. Violence ensued against the Jews. The 5,000 soldiers stationed in the town did nothing to quell it. When the smoke cleared, 49 Jews had been killed, 500 were injured; 700 homes looted and destroyed, 600 businesses and shops looted, 2,000 families left homeless. Later it was discovered that the child had been murdered by relatives and the suicide was unrelated to the Jews.

1903: The Okhrana, the Russian secret police in the reign of Czar Nicholas II, plagiarized an 1864 political satire and an anti-Semitic 1868 novel to form a document titled *Protocols of the Learned Elders of Zion.* Though entirely fictional, the publication purported to be the records of a secret Jewish society aiming to take over the world, "to subjugate and exterminate the Christians."

The Protocols of the Learned Elders of Zion

The Okhrana used the *Protocols* in a propaganda campaign associated with massacres of the Jews. These were known as the Czarist Pogroms of 1905.

The *Protocols* was translated into multiple languages and disseminated throughout the world. In the United States, it was published in 1920 in *The Dearborn Independent,* a Michigan newspaper started by Henry Ford mainly to attack Jews and Communists. Even after *The Protocols* was exposed as a complete forgery in 1921, the *Independent* continued to cite it as evidence of an alleged Jewish threat until at least 1927.

Henry Ford commented on February 17, 1921: "The only statement I care to make about the *Protocols* is that they fit in with what is going on. They are sixteen years old, and they have fitted the world situation up to this time. They fit it now."

Adolf Hitler later used *Protocols* in *Mein Kampf* to rationalize his assault against the Jews during World War II: "To what extent the whole existence of this people is based on a continuous lie is shown incomparably by *The Protocols of the Wise Men of Zion....*"

The Protocols of the Wise Men of Zion was sold via Wal-Mart's online bookstore until September 21, 2004.

1915: 600,000 Jews were forcibly moved from the western borders of Russia towards the interior. About 100,000 died of exposure or starvation.

1917: In the civil war following the Bolshevik Revolution of 1917, the reactionary White Armies made extensive use of *The Protocols* to incite widespread slaughters of Jews. 200,000 Jews were murdered in the Ukraine alone.

1920: The defeat of Germany in World War I and the continuing economic difficulties were blamed on the "Jewish influence" in that country. One anti-Semitic poster preserved from that era shows a German, presumably Christian woman, a Jewish man with distorted facial features, a coffin and the word "Deutschland" (Germany).

1925: Hitler published *Mein Kampf,* writing: "Today I believe that I am acting in accordance with the will of the Almighty Creator; by defending myself against the Jew, I am fighting for the work of the Lord."

The "Christianity" of Adolf Hitler
From his speech in Munich on April 12, 1922

" . . . I say: My feelings as a Christian point me to my Lord and Savior as a fighter. It points me to the man who once in loneliness, surrounded only by a few followers, recognized these Jews for what they were and summoned men to the fight against them and who, God's truth!…was greatest not as sufferer but as fighter.

"Today, after two thousand years, with deepest emotion I recognize more profoundly than ever before-- the fact that it was for this that He had to shed His blood upon the Cross. As a Christian I have no duty to allow myself to be cheated, but I have the duty to be a fighter for truth and justice. And as a man I have the duty to see to it that human society does not suffer the same catastrophic collapse as did the civilization of the ancient world some two thousand years ago-- a civilization which was driven to its ruin through this same Jewish people.

"And if there is anything which could demonstrate that we are acting rightly, it is the distress which daily grows. For as a Christian I have also a duty to my own people. And when I look on my people I see it work and work and toil and labor, and at the end of the week it has only for its wage wretchedness and misery. When I go out in the morning and see these men standing in their queues and look into their pinched faces, then I believe I would be no Christian, but a very devil, if I felt no pity for them, if I did not, as did our Lord two thousand years ago, turn against those by whom today this poor people is plundered and exploited."

1930: Persecution of Jews commenced in Hitler's Germany, with the inception of the systematic destruction of six million

Jews (including 1.5 million children) throughout Nazi-occupied Europe.

1933: Hitler became chancellor in Germany. On April 1, Julius Streicher organized a one-day boycott of all Jewish-owned business in the country. This was the start of continuous oppression by the Nazis culminating in the Holocaust (also known as *Shoah*). Jews were barred from civil service, legal professions and universities, were not allowed to teach in schools and could not be editors of newspapers.

1934: Various laws were enacted in Germany to force Jews out of schools and professions.

1935: The Nazis passed the Nuremberg Laws restricting citizenship to those of "German or related blood." Jews became stateless non-citizens.

1936: Cardinal Hloud of Poland urged Catholics to boycott all Jewish businesses.

1938: On November 9, the Nazi government in Germany sent storm troopers, the SS and the Hitler Youth on a pogrom that killed 91 Jews, injured hundreds, burned 177 synagogues and looted 7,500 Jewish stores. Broken glass could be seen everywhere, resulting in this event becoming known as *Kristallnacht*, the Night of Broken Glass.

Kristallnacht

The Germans had been looking for a way to get rid of their Jews. They began with the Polish Jews, rounding them up on the cold, rainy night of October 28, 1938. 17,000 Polish Jews were beaten across the border into Poland.

Herschel Grynszpan, a seventeen-year-old Polish Jew living in Paris, had parents who were part of the German-forced Jewish exile. This earnest young man felt the need to show the world what was happening to the Jews in Germany. Acquiring a gun, he walked into the German Embassy in Paris and shot the first man he saw, an Embassy official named Ernst Von Rath. Von Rath died, and this triggered a purportedly spontaneous uprising against the Jews. (The furor actually had been planned for some time and Von Rath's death was the pretext to put the plan into action.)

"On the nights of November 9 and 10, gangs of Nazi youth roamed through Jewish neighborhoods, breaking windows of Jewish businesses and homes, burning synagogues, and looting. In all, 101 synagogues were destroyed and almost 7,500 Jewish businesses were destroyed. 26,000 Jews were arrested and sent to concentration camps; Jews were physically attacked and beaten and 91 died.

"Three days later, on November 12, top Nazi leaders held a meeting to determine the economic impact of the damage they had caused and to discuss further measures to be taken against the Jews. The economic impact of the damages from Kristallnacht as well as the resulting insurance claims to be paid out covering the destruction was massive. This same Nazi leadership who had instigated and carried out this hideous attack decided that any insurance money due the Jews would be confiscated by "the State," and the Jews would also be billed for the cost of the damages – over one billion German marks."

Kristallnacht turned out to be a crucial turning point in German strategy regarding the Jews, and is considered by many as the actual beginning of the Holocaust.

The Philadelphia Inquirer
PUBLIC LEDGER

JEWS NOW FINED FOR NAZI RIOTS

100 Are Assessed For Damage Done To Stores by Mobs

1938: Hitler reinvigorated centuries-old church law, ordering all Jews to wear a yellow Star of David as identification. Thousands of Jews were allowed to leave Germany-- only after they had relinquished all their assets to the government.

1939: The Holocaust, the Shoah-- the systematic extermination of Jews in Germany-- began. The process would not end until 1945, with the conclusion of World War II. Approximately six million Jews (1.5 million of them children), 400,000 Roma (Gypsies) and others were slaughtered. Some were killed by death squads; others were slowly killed in trucks with carbon monoxide; others were gassed in large groups in Auschwitz, Dachau, Sobibor, Treblinka and other extermination camps. Officially, the Holocaust was described by the Nazis as subjecting Jews "to special treatment" or as a "final solution of the Jewish question."

1939: The *St. Louis*, a German luxury cruise ship, arrived in Havana, crammed with 906 German Jewish refugees escaping the Nazi threat. The ship was denied the right to dock in Cuba. Days later, the U.S. Immigration office refused the *St. Louis* permission to dock in Florida. The ship was forced to return to Germany where certain death awaited many of the refugees.

Voyage of the St. Louis

Sailing so close to Florida that they could see the lights of Miami, passengers on the *St. Louis* cabled President Franklin D. Roosevelt, asking for refuge.

Roosevelt never answered the cable.

The State Department and the White House had already decided not to let the refugees enter the United States. A State Department telegram sent to a passenger stated that the passengers must "await their turns on the waiting list and then qualify for and obtain immigration visas before they may be admissible into the United States." In other words, visas could have been granted to the passengers only by delaying them for the thousands of German Jews who already had applied for them.

President Roosevelt could have issued an executive order to admit additional refugees, but chose not to do so for a variety of *political* reasons. Primary among them was a 1939 Roper Poll that reported 53% of the US population considered Jews to be "different" and that they "should be separated." The majority of the citizens within the "Christian" nation of the United States of America wanted nothing to do with the Jews of Europe.

1940: The Vichy government of France collaborated with Nazi Germany by freezing about 80,000 Jewish bank accounts. During the next four years, they deported about 76,000 Jews to Nazi death camps; only about 2,500 would survive.

It was not until 1995 that French President Jacques Chirac was able to admit that the state bore a heavy share of responsibility in the mass roundups and deportations of Jews, as well as in the property and asset seizures that were carried out with the active help of the Vichy regime.

1941: The Holocaust Museum in Washington, DC, estimates that 13,000 Jews died on June 19, 1941, during a pogrom in Bucharest, Romania. It was ordered by the pro-Nazi Romanian regime of Marshal Ion Antonescu.

1941: Polish citizens in Jedwabne, Poland, killed hundreds of Jews by beating them to death or burning them alive in a barn. The role played by Polish citizens was suppressed for nearly six decades until the publication of *Neighbours,* a book by a Polish émigré historian Jan Tomasz Gross. After the book's release in 2000, the Polish government launched an investigation. "The role of the Poles was decisive in conducting the criminal act," prosecutor Radoslaw Ignatiew said. The book sparked national soul-searching among Poles, many of whom could not believe that anybody but the Nazis would have committed the atrocity.

1942: At the Wannsee conference, the Nazi leaders of Germany decided on "the final solution of the Jewish question," which was the attempt to exterminate every Jew in Europe. From July 28 to 31, almost 18,000 Russian inhabitants of the Minsk ghetto in what is now Belarus were exterminated. This was in addition to 5,000 to 15,000 who had been massacred in earlier pogroms in that city. This was just one of many such pogroms during World War II.

1945: The Holocaust ended as the Allied Forces overran the Nazi death camps.

Even though World War II ended the year before, anti-Semitic pogroms continued, particularly in Poland, with the deaths of many Jews.

2007: Former President Jimmy Carter's *Palestine: Peace, Not Apartheid* was published.

2012: The Presbyterian Church's USA General Assembly voted overwhelmingly 457 to 180 in favor of boycotting products made by Jewish companies in Judea and Samaria and called upon all nations to prohibit the importing of the products. A similar measure passed at the United Methodist general assembly earlier the same year.

Christian anti-Semitism is still very much alive – and the Jewish people are painfully aware of it.

Answering the Question
"Does the Christian community have the patience for us?"

Rabbi Isaac faintly smiled and asked again, "Does the Christian community have the patience for us?"

My answer at the time was, "Rabbi, we are not waiting for anything from the Jewish people. There is no need for patience on our part concerning the Jewish people."

Since the time of this workshop I have had many opportunities to reconsider Rabbi Isaac's fears about the new Christian Zionist support.

The Jews feel a solidarity with their past, as if they are all on the same train. Throughout history, Christian societies have derailed the Jewish train over and over again. Christians generally sense no such relationship or connection with our history. Most don't even know there is a train.

This ponderous question concerning "Christian patience" should reverberate with an overwhelming and searing conviction if we allow ourselves to embrace even the slightest amount of culpability in light of our Christian history with the Jewish people.

Not until we are willing to step into the insane hopelessness of being on the Jewish side of this horrendous experience, not until we imagine being maligned and cursed for over 1,900 years as the assassins of the Christian Jesus, not until we envision our own spouse, brother, sister, mother, father or child bound to the burning stakes of the Christian Inquisition, not until we have allowed ourselves to feel our fourteen-year-old daughter ripped from our arms and shoved into a parade of beautiful children who will be raped by ravenous Nazi officer pedophiles in the "Christian" nation of Germany…it is not until then that we might begin to understand the true horror of the rabbi's question.

How disoriented, how battered the historic Christian curse has left the Jewish people in their dealings with our faith. Even with the blessed bounty of their God-given brilliance and resilience, they have been forced into a coma of self-preservation when trying to reconcile this new Christian love for them with the history of those who also carried the cross.

Does the Christian community have the patience for us?

Is the answer not appallingly evident? It is we Christians, with broken hearts and bowed heads who must beseech every Jew we have the privilege of knowing: "Does the Jewish community have the patience for *us?*"

MARTINVS LVTHERVS *Theologus*
Natus Iflebiæ anno 1483. *obijt in patria anno* 1546.

Wenflaus Hollar fecit.   Ioan. Meÿffens exc. Antverni.

Question 2

"Do Christians still hate us because we don't believe in Jesus?"

Standard Christian Answer:

"Hate you? We don't hate you! How did you ever get such a crazy idea that we hated you? We love you and want you to know that!" ...and the 'Jesus talk' begins.

The Founders Group

The Founders Group is composed of a select number of prominent citizens, each the founder of a successful business. This energetic, creative group offers substantive opportunities to meet and socialize with people who can play a role in shaping the Jewish community and the wider world. Guest speakers at the philanthropy meetings have included: Senator Joseph Lieberman, Dr. Henry Kissinger, Prime Minister Ehud Barak, Steven Spielberg, Dr. Charles Krauthammer, Congressman Eric Cantor, Irshad Manji (author of *The Trouble with Islam*), Hala Mustafa (a leader of Arab reform), Martin Kramer (author of *Ivory Towers on Sand*), and other prominent philanthropists, political figures, and scholars.

I had no idea who these mysterious Founders Group people were until returning home and researching some of those I met during the summit. For instance, all I knew about Bernie (with whom I shared a number of meals and many long conversations) was that he once "dabbled in the hardware business." My curiosity about this dear man was piqued, however, during one of the morning sessions when his Jewish friends gathered around and announced that they would be sitting Shiva with him.

> *For My Christian Readers:*
>
> *Shiva* is an emotionally and spiritually healing time where friends come together with a Jewish family in their time of mourning, and comfort them with short visits, "Shiva calls."

There was something bizarre about the manner in which Bernie's dear friends were offering their comfort: They were all snickering and laughing! I inched closer to this morbid group of *friends* gathered around him, learning that they were mourning-- the death of *his whale shark!* Now understanding their lightheartedness, I could not help but wonder, "What kind of guy has a pet whale shark, and where in the world does he keep it?"

I heard Bernie quietly groan as he asked one of the still giggling women standing next to him, "How did you hear about it so soon?"

She replied, "It was on CNN this morning!"

Several days later I discovered that my very gracious weekend host, Bernie, was actually Bernard – Bernard Marcus, one of the founders of Home Depot! His pet whale shark was found floating dorsal fin down in the gorgeous downtown Atlanta, Georgia aquarium he had built and generously donated to the city.

It was such an honor to have been asked to share my personal testimony and love for the Jewish people with Bernie and the other members of The Founders Group.

I had just finished my presentation to the group when a Jewish woman startled me by asking, *"Do you still hate us because we don't believe in Jesus?"*

I was stunned, and for a moment speechless.

"What?" I hesitated, in disbelief. "Do we hate you?" Unable to grasp the question, I continued, "Do you actually think that there are Christians today who hate you because you don't believe what we believe about Jesus?"

Her immediate response was a guarded, nervous nod of her head, followed by a whispered, "Well, yes."

In dismay I quickly locked eyes with the two Jewish men standing next to her and inquired, "Is this something you've ever believed? That Christians actually hate you because you don't believe in Jesus?"

"Sure," they both answered, as nonchalantly as if I had asked, "Would you like to go grab a sandwich?"

Tears filled my eyes and rolled down my cheeks. "I am so sorry," I offered them.

Why Would Jews Believe Christians Hate Them?

I had been active as a Christian Zionist for over two decades, and the thought had never crossed my mind, nor had the question been presented to me quite as directly or with such sincerity, but it is a question many Jews ponder. Christians must deeply consider why it remains a question to Jews and when asked, answer with the understanding and humility such a question demands.

Immediately after this occurrence, I asked my buddy David Brog, the Executive Director of Christians United for Israel (CUFI), if this was a genuine concern on the hearts of the Jewish community.

For My Christian Readers:

David Brog is a conservative Jew serving as Executive Director of Christians United for Israel. David lives and writes in Washington, D.C., and worked in the United States Senate for seven years, rising to be chief of staff to a senior U.S. senator and staff director of the Senate Judiciary Committee. Prior to his time on Capitol Hill, David practiced corporate law in Tel Aviv, Israel and Philadelphia, Pennsylvania. David is a graduate of Princeton University and Harvard Law School. He is the author of **Standing With Israel, Why Christians Support The Jewish State** and **Defending the Faith.** I pray that these two books become required reading in all of our Christian seminary campuses. I implore you, as well, to read them.

"Well, Victor," David began with a wry smile, signifying that he was getting ready both to educate me and boot me across the room like a soccer ball. "If you remember, you guys hunted us down and killed us for quite a few years because we didn't believe what you did about Jesus. So for a lot of Jews, yeah... that kind of left us with the impression you don't like us much," he explained.

"Well, when you say it like that . . ." I almost answered. But I suddenly realized that for Jews-- it *is* like that.

A Story About My Father

Before suggesting how Christians answer this question, I need to have you know my remarkable father and about an event that changed his life-- and mine.

My dad, Alfred Miroslav Bohumil Styrsky, loved my precious mom, his children, his God and just about every single life form upon our planet. He was enamored with the heavens, the stars, and

I'm sure he would have loved extraterrestrials had he ever met one. He did not love injustice, war, bigotry, or religious arrogance of any kind.

I actually look a lot like my dad and cannot help but think about him as I see him looking back at me in the mirror every day! When loving my own children and grandchildren, I try my best to emulate the cosmic father he was to me.

For Father's Day, 1987, I wrote the following song in Dad's honor.

I hope it will help you understand his profound influence on my life.

My Friend, My Father, My Dad

I can remember so many adventures in life with my father.
And when I was little, it all was so simple 'cause I have the best
dad ever.
And now that I'm older, he still hasn't changed;
There's nobody else like that man!

My friend, my father, my dad.

I learned from him how to fish and to swim and to say, "I'm
sorry."
We'd travel through time, as I'd climb on his knee and he'd tell me
all his stories.
And I learned from him that a man can cry, and giving means all
that you have.

My friend, my father, my dad.

Remember his words-- stay on the path
He taught you from your youth -- for it will keep you.

Now I'm a father and it sure is harder to lead than to follow.
And yet there are times when I still hear my Dad's voice inside,
telling me where to go.
And when I see Jesus, I may be surprised He reminds me so much
of that man!

My friend, my father, my dad.

© V. Styrsky 1987

My Lutheran Upbringing

Until my early teens, I accompanied my dad and mom to church out of love and respect for them. Though raised in a Christian home, I did not come to faith until I was twenty years old. The memories of my childhood church experiences are best summarized by saying, "I pretty much detested the whole thing."

- The sermons-- ugh. I hated them.
- The Sunday clothes that I was straitjacketed into. Hated them.
- The circus organ music-- yuck.
- The liturgy-- snore, the "lethargy"!

Ah, the liturgy:

"I believe in God, the Father Almighty, Creator of heaven and earth. I believe in Jesus Christ, His only Son, our Lord. He was conceived by the power of the Holy Spirit and born of the Virgin Mary. He suffered under an unconscious pilot (Pontius Pilot actually-- but that was not what I heard!) *was crucified, died, and was buried."*

"What in the world was Jesus doing, suffering under an unconscious pilot?"

The Lutheran liturgy I endured as a child added nothing but confusion to my Sunday morning religious detention. I could not for the life of me figure out the image I had of Jesus gazing upon a pilot who had been knocked unconscious in a P-51 Mustang airplane, which apparently had crashed into a tree! Suffered under an unconscious pilot??

I just didn't get it.

I even remember the smell of the church, and I didn't like that, either. It was not the sweet, exciting and exotic aroma of incense, but the stale, musky smell of acute dullness.

I especially did not like the awkward and forced obligation of standing in line at the end of every service to shake hands with the stranger in a satin robe who had been preaching. This was the same man who, for the previous hour, had attempted over and over again to kill me with boredom. What in the world were my parents doing, making me shake his hand?

These memories are my childhood religious recollections mixed with the unspoken madness inherent in the confusion of worshiping somebody I could not see or understand.

But worshiping my dad was easy, and he was easy to understand – and I did worship him. One of my very earliest memories of life entails explaining to my four-year-old friends in Green Bay, Wisconsin, that my dad was the very first man on the earth. My dad was Adam.

He really was, to me.

My dad's accomplishments and his unconditional love for me merited his sacred position in my eyes. My dad was also a highly decorated P-51 Mustang fighter pilot during WWII. Enjoy here a page of excerpts from his personal journal briefly describing several of his missions.

Al Styrsky

England – The 354th Fighter Group
Alfred Miroslav Bohumil Styrsky and his mascot "Flak!"
WWII Branch of Service: U.S. Army Air Corps
P-51 Mustang fighter pilot in the 356th Fighter Squadron, 354th
Fighter Group. Flew 85 missions over France and Germany.
Posthumously awarded the Distinguished Flying Cross in 2004 for
his mission over Hanover, Germany on January 30, 1944.

"In November 1943, a dozen of my comrades and I arrived in England as pilot replacements to be joined to the well-established 354th Fighter Group based at Boxted. We were most fortunate to be placed in such a well- trained and outstanding group of flyers.

"On the 4th of July, the 356th was chosen to escort "Stars Look Down," carrying General Eisenhower and General "Pete" Quesada. While at cruising altitude I felt a hit from ground fire. I knew my plane was hit in the engine area and any moment I expected to see coolant boiling out. Keeping my eye on the gauge, I worried for a while. All appeared to be okay and I continued with the mission. No one else experienced any ground fire. Later my crew chief pointed out the marksmanship of the Jerry gunner. He must have had some eye. The hole in the engine cowling was ever so near to a vital coolant line.

"The news account of our harrowing mission on D-Day is enclosed. We escorted slow-flying C-47s towing gliders, under a two-thousand-foot ceiling, during darkness, with no lights in snug formation. Returning fighters from the invasion area added an additional touch of suspense. To further complicate matters, my engine began overheating. I found that I was able to keep the temperature normal by using the manual switch, although I was taking a chance that there might have been a small coolant leak. It worked out that I was able to complete that mission.

"By the end of October I had flown 84 combat missions and was placed on the list for rotation to the United States.

"This curtailed my combat flying. Being restless, I asked Operations (either Bob Brooks or Harry Fisk) to fly another mission. They were reluctant but finally relented and scheduled me for a dive-bombing mission of a railroad terminal. The cloudy weather hindered our mission severely. A break in the clouds made it possible to bomb the rail yard, but only one plane at a time, limited as we were by visibility restriction.

"In November, my departure time came. I bid a fond good-bye to my comrades whose wings and tails I had faithfully covered through many an ordeal. I had clung to their wings flying through thousands of feet of foul weather, caught heavy flak over the Rurh Industrial Space, had ground fire lace through our formations (at times the shells looking like snowballs, a strange and hard to believe phenomenon, usually occurring on a dive bombing run), our mortal bodies hurtling through a melee of planes, protecting my lead pilots' tails as they cavorted after a bandit.

"All of us drank of this cup of peril. To paraphrase a line from our Air Corps song, 'How we lived? God only knew.'

When I parted company of my ground crew and flying comrades that I had known for the past year, it was with mixed emotions. Glad to be going home and sad to be leaving these good friends. As Robert Brooks bid me good-bye, he told me that I would be submitted for a Distinguished Flying Cross."

The Betrayal of My Father

Within these most condensed of observations, I hope you can capture the essence of my remarkable father. I have opened this door of my heart to you so that you may more fully comprehend one final and perplexing story about his life.

This story is not one of bravery and valor but an account of betrayal he suffered through the actions of the US Air Force. It was a betrayal that would play a critical part in ending his life and changing mine in an amazing and wonderful way.

Operation Greenhouse

In 1951, Dad participated in the top-secret project, Operation Greenhouse, involving atomic weapon tests on Eniwetok, an island in the South Pacific. He recounted: "The first nuclear detonation was scheduled for April 8th, 1951. Volunteers were called for to fly an Air Force officer over the blast site for him to monitor the extent of radiation and pick up exposed film badges. I was chosen for the first shot, the flight to be made less than an hour after the blast. At the request of the monitor, I guided the plane right over the crater site at which point the monitor, alarmed by the sudden extreme readings on his hand-held radiation counter, shouted, 'Get us out of here!'"

My father writes, "At no time were we advised of the cumulative radiation exposure we had taken on our persons."

The United States Air Force buried my father's medical record, which noted the dangerous, and eventually deadly dose of radiation to which he had been exposed. They immediately removed him from Operation Greenhouse and sent him home, telling him that he should suffer no ill effects from the mission, other than possibly being sterile.

The family joke is that I was born almost exactly nine months from the day he came home to my mom. Realizing I am the fruit of radioactive spermatozoid has been very helpful to my friends and family as they try to understand me.

My father's health was gravely affected by this incident. Had he been informed of the deadly radiation dosage to which he had been exposed, there were medical procedures and precautions that could have benefited his life to a great extent. As it was, he suffered enormously because of the deceitful actions of the institution he trusted and courageously served. The institution that should have protected and honored my father had betrayed him.

A Life-Changing Confession and Apology

One day, several years before my dad passed away, he received a letter from a young officer in the United States Air Force. This honorable young man was not even alive during the Second World War but upon discovering the hidden medical records concerning this event at Eniwetok, he wrote an apology to my father. In the letter, he attempted to confess the sins that the US Air Force had committed against Dad (using military jargon, of course) and to ask him and our family for forgiveness.

My father was such a good and forgiving man and had never sought after this confession; yet the unexpected letter's content greatly uplifted his spirit.

This admission by the United States Air Force of their transgression against my father, and their recognition of the unjust suffering he endured as a result touched me in a very profound way.

As far as I am concerned, the U.S. Air Force has not done anything as righteous in its entire existence. How could I feel anything less?

The military's apology, although withheld for over forty years, somehow helped mend my personal wounds of grief and injustice concerning the matter.

The Lack of Christian Culpability

Just as the officer who wrote to my father identified with the failures of his military community members who served a generation before him, so the Hebrew prophet Nehemiah identified with-- and sought forgiveness for-- the sins of the Israelites from the generation past:

Nehemiah 1:6,7

I confess the sins we Israelites, including myself and my father's house, have committed against you. We have acted very wickedly toward you. We have not obeyed the commands, decrees and laws you gave your servant Moses.

In an account recorded in the book of 2 Samuel: 21, we find God requiring confession of sin and restitution from King David for the sins of a previous generation. There was a famine during David's reign that lasted for three years, so David asked the Lord about it. And the Lord said, "The famine has come because Saul and his family are guilty of murdering the Gibeonites."

So the king summoned the Gibeonites. They were not part of Israel but were all that was left of the nation of the Amorites. The people of Israel had sworn not to kill them, but Saul, in his zeal for Israel and Judah, had tried to wipe them out.

> David asked them, "What can I do for you? How can I make amends so that you will bless the Lord's people again?"

> "Well, money can't settle this matter between us and the family of Saul," the Gibeonites replied. "Neither can we demand the life of anyone in Israel."

> "What can I do then?" David asked. "Just tell me and I will do it for you."

> Then they replied, "It was Saul who planned to destroy us, to keep us from having any place at all in the territory of

Israel. So let seven of Saul's sons be handed over to us, and we will execute them before the Lord at Gibeon, on the mountain of the Lord."

"All right," the king said, "I will do it."

2 Samuel 21: 9, 13, 14

...The men of Gibeon executed the seven sons on the mountain before the Lord. So all seven of them died together at the beginning of the barley harvest. Then the king ordered that their bones be buried in the tomb of Kish, Saul's father, at the town of Zela in the land of Benjamin. After that, God ended the famine in the land.

"How can we Christians today explain doing anything less than identifying with the sins of our past generations toward the Jewish people?"

Though we were not present during the Crusades or the Inquisition, it is very doubtful that we would have fought against the Christian insanity of those times. During the time of Martin Luther, in all probability we would have followed in lockstep behind his anti-Semitic theology, as did the mesmerized Hitler Youth behind the lethal wake of Adolf Hitler.

We can begin to make amends today for what was done then.

Though we almost certainly would have joined mute voices with the deadly silent church choir during the horrors of the Shoah, we can today resolve to stand up and speak out in opposition to the anti-Semitic war being waged against the Jewish people.

For My Christian Readers:

Holocaust is from the Greek *holokauston* meaning "burnt whole" or "that which is completely burnt" and refers to Hitler's genocide of 6 million Jews (almost 2/3 of the European Jewish population). The Hebrew *Shoah*, meaning "total and tragic annihilation that surpassed everything" is the term used by many Jews when speaking of this unspeakably wicked moment in history, as it more accurately describes the devastation caused by it.

Understanding the Question

We will not wholly understand or know the pain of another unless we have experienced the same suffering. The most empathetic observer is still incapable of fully comprehending the intimate effects of an affliction upon the one enduring it.

Through the circumstance in my father's life, and through the confession of a young, gallant and godly officer serving in the US Air Force, I have tasted a portion of the unjust suffering as well as the worthy vindication of my dad. His hardship and the repentance of the U.S. Air Force are, of course, in no way proportionate to the affliction of the Jewish people and the need of repentance from the Christian community, but this very personal experience changed my life.

Until these events had touched our family, I had never considered how appalling it is for a Jew to be lunged at with a Jesus pamphlet by a Christian stranger claiming "love" for him. I believe I am beginning to understand how we provoke the Jews' disdain from our mechanical missionary attempts that have so little to do with the love of Jesus.

Unless we embrace the appalling historic suffering the Jewish people have endured from those who have claimed faith in Christ, we can never begin to comprehend the justified Jewish dismay at our unsolicited attempts to witness to them.

In the spirit of this understanding, I pray that the efforts of Christian Zionists may begin a new history of support, encouragement, and blessing to the hearts of our Jewish friends.

For My Christian Readers:

If my analogy and conclusions seem harsh to you, I ask you to present these thoughts to your Jewish friends for their perspective. I believe they will confirm my thoughts. If you have no Jewish friends, then please keep reading this book!

Answering the question:
"Do Christians still hate us because we don't believe in Jesus?"

I pray that more and more Christians will search out and understand why this ominous question would weigh upon a Jewish heart.

I pray that the zealous Christian community begins to realize just how surreal we appear when preaching to-- rather than compassionately listening to-- the people who have been destroyed under our banner for the last 1,900 years.

Consider answering the question using the thoughts within the following response:

"The abominable sins that have been committed against you over the last 1,900 years from those calling themselves Christians are the most wicked in the history of mankind. There is no restitution we can offer that could ever begin to compensate for our crimes against you and I ask God and you for forgiveness."

You must understand that this moment may be awkward. Very few Christians have ever asked Jews for forgiveness. We have chosen to keep the records of our culpability ignorantly buried or ignored, and have remained unrighteously indifferent to our Christian sins against them.

Your startled inquirer may also try to explain to you that in the Jewish concept of forgiveness, the living cannot forgive on behalf of the dead. In an inexplicable way however, I believe he has granted your request immediately upon hearing your words. You can finish answering the question by stating:

"Of course we don't hate you. We believe that you are the beloved of HaShem and the apple of His eye, and I bless you in the Name of the God of Abraham, Isaac, and Jacob."

Question 3

"What is your real agenda in reaching out to the Jews?"

Standard Christian Answer:

"We just love Jews and want to help you understand that" ...and the 'Jesus talk' begins.

During the Q & A session of our Sunday-afternoon seminar hosted by "NEVER AGAIN: Christians Standing With Israel," a middle-aged Christian woman asked our distinguished Jewish guest speaker, "How does it make you guys feel knowing that the only reason Christians are helping you is to bring you to believe in Jesus?"

Our guest speaker caught the knuckleball question she flung at his heart and, without a blink, set it down with the tenderness of a father tucking his little child into bed. God bless the Jews for their enormous longsuffering with us.

For my Christian readers:

"NEVER AGAIN: Christians Standing With Israel" was a Sacramento-based initiative headed by Randy Neal, the CUFI Western States Coordinator. After the Holocaust and following the birth of the nation of Israel, Jews cried out, "NEVER AGAIN! Never again will we live in the fear of being hunted down and killed. Never again, never again!" As Christian Zionists, we stand with the Jewish people to assure them that never again will they stand alone to face the terror of anti-Semitism.

We describe these types of incidents as having a *very high cringe factor*, especially in light of the clear announcement at the commencement of all our events that we have a non-conversionary agenda. We have much work ahead of us to educate the Christian masses on expressing unconditional love for the Jewish people.

This biblically commanded love is an act of adoration and obedience to God, and is a *Kiddush Hashem* for us to perform! This wellmeaning woman had not yet graduated from our makeshift Christian Zionist academy… or possibly arrived late and missed our mission statement, was hard of hearing, or is just one of the legions of unaware *mashugenas* in our faith community.

For my Christian readers:

Kiddush HaShem is Hebrew for "sanctification of the Name of God."

Mashugena is Yiddish for "crazy" or "goofball."

Getting the Jews Back to Israel: A Jewish Urban Myth

I was on the phone with the personal assistant to Mayor Willie Brown during his long reign over San Francisco politics. The woman was an active pro-Israel Jewish zealot and had recently become a friend through my work with pro-Israel Christians. "You really should publish a paper on Christian theology involving your relationship to the Jewish people," my new ally suggested.

"What exactly do you recommend it would cover?" I asked.

"Well, you know that most Jews believe that the only reason Christians are wanting to stand with us is to get us to make *aliyah* so that Jesus can return," she remarked matter-of-factly.

For my Christian readers:

Aliyah, which literally means "going up," is the Jewish legal right of return to the land of Israel.

"Wait a minute," I asked, trying to replay the answer she had just given me. "You think we believe that we have to get the Jews to Israel so that Jesus can return?" I clumsily restated her question.

The connection of those two thoughts was absolutely alien to me, thus my stumbling attempt to reiterate them. Even though I had been an active pro-Israel Christian for many years, this was the very first time I had ever been let in on this secret information concerning my "real" interest in the Jewish people.

Since this discovery, I have addressed many Jewish audiences of all ages and have been completely shocked to find that this belief amongst the Jewish people is held as undoubted truth. Whenever I ask my Jewish friends where they first heard this story, they always answer, "From a Jew."

The reason Jews have only heard this story from other Jews is because it is nowhere to be found in Christian theology. Evangelicals have no eschatological teaching (end-of-days theology) that requires all Jews to be back in the land of Israel for a Messianic visitation. Neither do evangelical Christians believe that there is anything we can do to hasten the return (or the first visit, as my Jewish friends believe) of Messiah.

Mainstream Christian theology has *always* taught that the return of Christ was imminent.

James 5:7-9

"Be patient, then, brothers, until the Lord's coming. See how the farmer waits for the land to yield its valuable crop and how patient he is. You too, be patient and stand firm, because the Lord's coming is near." --James, brother of Jesus

Mainstream Christian theology teaches there is a day and an hour when Christ will return and we don't know, nor can we know, nor can we speed up or hinder that predetermined and appointed time.

Mark 13:31-33

Heaven and earth will pass away, but My words will not pass away. But of that day or hour no one knows, not even the angels in heaven, nor the Son, but the Father alone. Take heed; keep on the alert, for you do not know when the appointed time will come.

--Jesus of Nazareth

Evangelical Christian theology concerning the coming of Christ is unified on the following points:

1) A pre-ordained date for the event has already been secured.
2) Only God the Father knows the time.
3) The coming of Messiah is imminent.
4) This appointed time cannot and will not be hastened nor detained by our activities or lack thereof.

The early church believed the coming of Messiah was imminent.

Philippians 4:4-5

"Always be full of joy in the Lord. I say it again – rejoice!
Let everyone see that you are considerate in all you do.
Remember, the Lord is coming soon." Apostle Paul

Messiah and the Rebirth of the Nation of Israel

Do Christians believe that the great turmoil in the world today and the May 14, 1948 miracle rebirth of the nation of Israel have Messianic implications? Yes, but most of this is from our study of the Jewish prophets in the Bible. The Torah, the Talmud, the Jewish sages and many of rabbis of today present the same view!

Haggai 2:6

During the ingathering of the exiles to Israel, a short time before the future Final Redemption, the heavens and earth will shake.

Jewish commentary on this verse from the Abarbanel, speaking of the Messianic era:

The Abarbanel, Mashmiya Yishuah, Mivaser 13.2

"This is a hint of the upheaval and confusion throughout the world. And in this place, the Land of Israel, I will give peace," says the Lord of Hosts.

For my Christian readers:

Rabbi Yitzchak Abarbanel (1437-1508) is known simply as "The Abarbanel." A descendant of the House of King David, he is among the most revered of Jewish Bible commentators and thinkers.

A Night to Honor Israel

As the California Director for Christians United for Israel, my responsibilities include gathering California Christian supporters of Israel and assisting them in hosting events called "A Night to Honor Israel" in their home cities. In the early years of CUFI, we were hosting over 50 pro-Israel events a year, all across the nation, from the Detroit, Michigan "Night to Honor Israel," which was a gathering of over 6,500 people, to the Berkeley, California, celebration (yes, we held a "Night to Honor Israel" in Berkeley!)

We now hold *over 50 events a month,* including pro-Israel events in Africa, Scotland, and Canada. (Please go to: www.CUFI.org to view our monthly calendar of events!)

I now have many precious Jewish friendships because of my affiliation with CUFI, and an especially dear friend is my buddy, Avi. When I first met Avraham (Avi) Alpert, he was the extremely gifted cantor of Sacramento's Mosaic Law Congregation, a constituent of the United Synagogue of Conservative Judaism.

Avi loves the Torah; he loves the God of Abraham, Isaac, and Jacob; and he loves the challenges of being an observant Jew. From his point of view, devoted dedication is not negotiable in his book, or in the Torah.

Avi and I first met after the Sacramento Night to Honor Israel that CUFI hosted in 2006. He had been asked to sing the national anthem, and I was honored to be the emcee for the evening. My Christian music ministry, Wild Branches, participated in the event as well.

The Sacramento Crest Theatre was packed with close to a thousand guests from the Jewish and Christian communities. We were all treated to an extraordinary outpouring of the Spirit of God: for almost three hours we laughed, cried, sang, and even danced in the aisles during this holy convocation. Avi and I embraced at the conclusion of the evening. We agreed that we needed to get together for coffee in the very near future.

Avi wrote an article for his synagogue's monthly newsletter, *The Scroll*, which follows. I ask that you explore his thoughts concerning the effect our Sacramento Night to Honor Israel had upon his life.

Mosaic Law's November Scroll from: The Cantor's Voice.

EMOTIONAL SINGING

Can singing the Star Spangled Banner be a life-changing experience? Everyone knows the words and sings along.

Most Americans probably have this anthem committed to memory. Yet it is a tremendous honor to be asked to lead such a song. I recently accepted an invitation to sing our national anthem at the Crest Theatre. It was the kickoff to an evening entitled "A Night to Honor Israel" by CUFI (Christians United for Israel). This sold-out event and all of its sincere emotional singing and presentations unexpectedly kept tears streaming down my cheeks. After singing, "and the home of the brave," I slowly began to realize how monumental it was to be legitimized as an observant Jew and as a member of the kley ko-desh, the Jewish clergy, by religious Christians.

Last year, Rabbi Taff told us the story of the Chief Rabbi of Rome who was invited by the Pope to the Vatican and turned down the invitation as it was during Shemini Atseret. The Chief Rabbi would be observing God's commandment in the Torah to abstain from creative work on the holiday. Our rabbi reminded us that not so long ago, if a rabbi or any Jew was asked to go to the Vatican, they went (for fear of their life). We live in a different world today.

Christians: Catholics, Protestants, and especially Evangelicals treat Jews with honor.

While sitting at the CUFI event, listening to music and speeches that were orchestrated in an utmost respectful manner, I shed tears. These Christians proved with their voices and their videos that they want nothing more than to bless God's Chosen People. They are truly pained by the past atrocities perpetrated against Jews in the name of Christianity. They acknowledge our relationship with Hashem and want only to support us and our State of Israel.

These are wonderful times. Jews who practice Judaism are being supported by Christians. Faith groups are feeling less threatened by others and are more willing to see value beyond their own. Members of the clergy are reaching out to colleagues who believe differently, teaching love and singing together. I pray that all of the religions of the world will begin to bless the Jews and bless the tiny State of Israel.

Let us all make music of thanksgiving together.

--Hazzan Avraham Alpert

Jew and Gentile Friendship

Starbucks has become a universal neutral location for many first dates and business propositions. On October 5, 2006, Avi and I were about to experience both. I arrived fifteen minutes late and spotted him sitting outside sporting a fedora and a suit coat, looking like a million bucks. Wearing my stock California-pastor-jeans-and-T-shirt, running shoes (sans socks), and enough gel in my hair to withstand a gale, I realized I had probably underdressed for the occasion and felt like a "Cinderfella" who never got the dress-code memo for the ball.

Avi got up to greet me. As soon as we both sat down, I found my new acquaintance had a lot on his mind. His heart was bursting with a recent discovery he had made, and his zeal to enlighten me was burning a hole in his spirit and thoughts.

"I've been reading a very interesting book, Pastor Styrsky," Avi formally announced. "It's written by an evangelical Christian and is called *Misquoting Jesus*. Have you ever heard of it?" he asked.

"I haven't," I answered. But by the name of the book I assumed it was one of many, released every few years purporting to have the real goods on Jesus or the secret location of his first pair of sandals.

Avi let me know in no uncertain terms that the New Testament was (using his words) "a bunch of malarkey!" He explained to me his belief that the Greek documents claiming to contain the words of Christ are filled with more errors, additions, and subtractions than there are words in that entire document! (This is a belief that Avi continues to hold.)

I listened intently and loved every word Avi shared with me. "Now here is a guy with some chutzpah!" I smiled to myself.

> *For my Christian readers:*
> Chutzpah is from a Yiddish word meaning "intestinal fortitude."

I interrupted my impassioned friend a couple of times for clarification, and, when he brought his case to a close, I answered him.

"Avi, I'll grant you that the New Testament is a bunch of malarkey," I conceded. "I don't believe it is, but for the sake of this discussion, I'll give you that," I finished my brief opening statement.

"I don't need the New Testament to support my Christian faith. It's you guys who've sent me running after the carpenter from Nazareth. The Hebrew Scriptures – the only Bible the early church had are what convinced me Yeshua is the guy!"

> *For my Christian readers:*
> 'Jesus,' is transliterated from the Hebrew name Yeshua – the actual name He was known by while on earth. The word means 'salvation.'

And with my volley shot back across his bow, off we went, whacking our religious convictions back and forth in an exhilarating Biblical ping-pong match. We stopped for a breather, frantically opening our cell phones to check the myriad calls that had tried to disrupt our tournament. Breaking into laughter from disbelief, we both realized that we had been "Torah-tussling" for almost two hours!

We shook hands, gave each other a brotherly hug, walked a few feet toward the parking lot and talked for at least another fifteen minutes when Avi offered a proposition: "Let's get together again and do something constructive. Let's talk about doing some music together!"

Now, this was constructive! I laughed, quickly agreeing to his offer and adding that more coffee was definitely in order.

An extraordinary and holy friendship had begun.

Avi and I have so much in common: our love of God, our love of God's people, our love of Torah, the love of our families, and the love of music that is created solely for the adoration of our Creator.

Along with my work as a pastor, I have served as a music director for over half my adult life. My musical background in no way includes any of the incredible and praiseworthy achievements that Avi listed on his resume. My eligibility for being a leader of song within the Christian community is only the qualification noted in the New Testament Greek Scriptures:

Luke 7:47
He who has been forgiven much, loves much.

I am humbly overqualified in this manner, but like Avi, I love worshiping the Lord of Hosts in song.

Avi joined my evangelical Christian band.

I often declare this in front of his Jewish buddies just to goad him and try to get a rise out of his rabbi. My wife and I bought him a shirt imprinted: "IT'S OK-- I'M WITH THE BAND."

To be more accurate, Avi sometimes sings with our music ministry, Wild Branches at "Night to Honor Israel" celebrations around the country. (Go to YouTube and type "Wild Branches" in the search setting to see and hear all of us performing together at the San Diego "Night to Honor Israel.")

Together we sing the songs of Zion from the Psalms and Hebrew prophets. Though I have been performing some of these songs for over twenty years, they did not sound complete until Avi brought his spiritual portion to the music.

For my Christian readers:

Revelation 15:3

They sing the song of Moses, the servant of God, and the song of the Lamb, saying: "Great and marvelous are Your works, Lord God Almighty! Just and true are Your ways, O King of the ages."

As our band finished its first set at one such event, I felt a tap on my shoulder. A handsome silver-haired gentleman with a large Star of David around his neck leaned towards me and whispered so as to not disturb those around us, "Is the Jewish man singing with your band messianic or a Jew?"

Whenever Avi sings with Wild Branches in front of Jewish audiences, we emphasize in our introductions that Avi is a Conservative Jewish cantor. Even with our explanations, the novelty of seeing and hearing an evangelical Christian band and a Jewish cantor perform together often leaves people a bit puzzled!

I smiled and answered the distinguished inquirer, "He's not a messianic Jew; he is a Jew-Jew!" He quickly made his way back to his wife seated in the middle of the packed auditorium. Out of the corner of my eye, I watched him explain my answer to her. Upon hearing the report, her face lit up with a beaming smile. I read her lips as she exclaimed, "How wonderful!"

I agree. How wonderful, indeed.

Avi and I continue to see each other often. We eat together and drink lots of coffee. I'll grab my grandson Samuel, and pick up Avi and his son Ezra, to spend the afternoon doing "man adventures" together with our boys. My wife and I recently helped Avi and his family move all their belongings into a new home they purchased. (You know you are a real friend when you get invited to help someone move on a Monday morning!)

Avi and I talk about being married, and we talk about the love and challenges we experience in raising our children. We talk about the sheep in our pastures and how they like to gnaw on their shepherds.

We talk about our dreams as men, and we talk about our faith as spiritual brothers. Avi gave me a Tanakh and together we plunge into the book's Divine streams of revelation.

For my Christian readers:

Judaism refers to the first five books of the Hebrew Bible as The Torah, or the Books of Moses. The entire "Old Testament" is called The Tanakh. When the Apostle Paul wrote about the power of the Word of God, he was referring to the Tanakh!

Hebrews 4:12

For the word of God is living and active. Sharper than any double-edged sword, it penetrates even to dividing soul and spirit, joints and marrow; it judges the thoughts and attitudes of the heart.

The New Testament was not recognized as being divinely inspired until 325 AD.

Sometimes in formal settings, often over the phone or in casual conversation, we take every opportunity to talk about our faith in the God of Abraham, Isaac, and Jacob. We explore the ways and mysteries of the Almighty, sharing our common and contrasting thoughts.

Avi is no more threatened by my convictions than I am by his. He is a Jew and I am a Christian; and we love, respect, and deeply care for each other. Some Christians reading this book who already have been speculating that I might be a heretic are now almost certain that I am.

Look: It's like Avi's team is the Arizona Cardinals and my team is the San Francisco 49ers, but we both love football and passionate discussion about it!

Saul, Paul-- and Avi

I can guess what some Christians are now thinking: "How can you call yourself an Evangelical Christian and not try to convert your poor lost friend Avi? If you really loved him, you would tell him about Jesus!"

Jesus?

Yes, of course, Avi and I have spoken about Jesus, and he knows exactly what I believe about Him. As a matter of fact, he knew what I believed about Jesus before we met and ever discussed the matter.

Rabbis and cantors have an exhaustive education in Hebrew and Aramaic. Many I have met are also conversant with the Greek language. All rabbis are well educated regarding the various aspects of religion and history, and why Jews rejected the Christian Gospels and Christianity in general. Some of them use their knowledge of the Greek language for their study of the Septuagint and their study of the New Testament. I know a number of rabbis who are more familiar with the New Testament than many Christians.

> *For my Christian readers:*
>
> The Septuagint is the name given to the Greek translation of the Jewish Scriptures which were translated between 300 and 200 BC. This translation was produced because many Jews living throughout the Roman Empire were beginning to lose their Hebrew language. Because "Septuagint" is a Latin word meaning "seventy," the belief is that seventy to seventy-two Jewish scholars were commissioned to carry out the task of translation. The Septuagint was also a source of the Old Testament for early Christians during the first few centuries AD. Many early Christians spoke and read Greek, so they relied on the Septuagint translation for most of their understanding of the Old Testament. The New Testament writers also relied heavily on the Septuagint, as a majority of Old Testament quotes cited in the New Testament are quoted directly from the Septuagint (others are quoted from the Hebrew texts). Some rabbis today study the New Testament in order to give answers to their Jewish congregants concerning our faith in Jesus and why they do not believe Him to be Messiah.
>
> Our Christian faith's "good news" historically has been forced upon the Jews with the edge of a sword, the end of a hanging rope, the hot blaze of a torch, and often with the callous toss of a tract.

And I know that Avi has considered the scriptures and does not have the same conclusions as I do regarding Mashiach.

For my Christian readers:

Mashiach or *Moshiach* is Hebrew for "Messiah," the "Anointed One," the Redeemer of Israel, who will appear in *B'Acharit Hayamim*, meaning at the "End of Days," to redeem Israel from its enemies and bring peace to all the earth. Jesus was/is not recognized as Messiah by the Jewish people because while on earth he did neither.

And let me clarify this as well: I have not yet, in my thirty-five years of believing in Christ, converted one person. And believe it or not, neither have you. We do not have the power required to grant the personal revelation of Almighty God to another soul. As Christians, we believe this is the exclusive work of our heavenly Father.

Matthew 16:12-17

When Jesus came to the region of Caesarea Philippi, he asked his disciples, "Who do people say the Son of Man is?"

They replied, "Some say John the Baptist; others say Elijah; and still others, Jeremiah or one of the prophets."

"But what about you?" he asked. "Who do you say I am?"

Simon Peter answered, "You are the Christ, the Son of the living God."

Jesus replied, "Blessed are you, Simon son of Jonah, for this was not revealed to you by man, but by my Father in heaven."

I Peter 3:15-16 is my "North Star" for sharing my personal convictions about Jesus with the Jewish people. I pray the instruction becomes your guidance as well. Historically, our words have been hollow and deadly for Jews.

I Peter 3:15,16

And if someone asks about your Christian hope, always be ready to explain it. But do this in a gentle and respectful way.

If someone asks.

It is Jesus' little brother James, who summarizes much of our Christian history with the Jewish people.

James 2

So you see, faith, unless it produces good deeds, is as dead and useless-- as a corpse.

Over coffee one morning, Avi and I were reading through the book of Genesis from the Stone Edition Hebrew Torah translation. If you do not have a Torah, find a Jewish friend and get one. The book is unbelievably rich in color, tone and dialogue. The Jews are pretty familiar with the Hebrew language, so reading from their Biblical translation is enlightening and a spiritual banquet for us Gentile Christian types!

Avi was sharing with me wisdom from the Jewish sages, and I was pointing out the portions where Christians see Messianic implications, when Avi shook his head and said, "Man, you guys see Messiah everywhere!"

I smiled at his comment and answered, "Yeah, we sure do."
"Get over it already!" he laughed.

For my Christian readers:
The Jewish sages are composed of the most prominent rabbis of the first and second centuries AD. Their commentaries concerning the Hebrew Scriptures are written in the Mishna and the Talmud. The Mishna pertains to the Jewish legal code as

interpreted from the Scriptures, and the writings of the Talmud explain how to study the Mishna. Jews rely on these writings for their deeper understanding of Old Testament theology, much as Christians refer to commentary on the Scriptures from pastors and teachers.

I am a Christian, and Avi is a Jew-- and we love each other. He is not my project, my lucky rabbit's foot (those who bless the Jews will be blessed, etc) or my target. He acknowledges the God of Abraham, God of Isaac, and God of Jacob as God alone and as His Heavenly Father. I do as well. If Avi and I have the same father, then that makes us brothers.

Saul was a Jew in the New Testament who loved Torah, yet he hated and persecuted the followers of Yeshua. Paul was undoubtedly, powerfully "witnessed to" by many of the followers of Jesus he persecuted. It had no effect upon his life. But God had no problem getting Saul's attention; and after He did, Saul became Paul, our beloved apostle.

If my New Testament faith is true, it must also include the faith that only God is able to reveal His son to my precious Jewish friend. Exceedingly able to do so considering that, unlike in Saul's case-- Avi loves me.

Answering the question:

"What is your real agenda in reaching out to the Jews?"

When asked by the Jewish people, "What is your real agenda in reaching out to the Jews," I sincerely hope more and more Christians will understand why we are being asked this question and will honestly answer, starting with the following portion of the book of Exodus Chapter 17 (from the Stone Edition Torah):

"Now Amalek came and fought with Israel in Rephidim. And Moses said to Joshua, 'Choose people for us and go do battle with Amalek. Tomorrow I will stand on the top of the hill with the rod of God in my hand.'

"So Joshua did as Moses said to him, to do battle with Amalek. And Moses, Aaron, and Hur went up to the top of the hill. It happened that when Moses held up his hand, Israel was stronger; and when he let down his hand, Amalek was stronger. But Moses's hands grew heavy; so they took a stone and put it under him, and he sat on it. And Aaron and Hur supported his hands, one on this side, and one on that side; and he remained with his hands in faithful prayer until sunset. So Joshua defeated Amalek and its people with the sword's blade. Moses built an altar and called its name 'HaShem is My Miracle.'"

And then we may finish answering their question.

HaShem often uses people to perform His miracles. Christian Zionists want to be part of the miracle He is doing with the Jewish people. We want to encourage you and join you in the battle against you.

We want to lift your hands; we want to be on this side of you and on that side of you. Never again will you walk alone. Never again will you say, 'There is no one for us.' We believe that you are the beloved of HaShem and the apple of His eye, and we bless you in the Name of the God of Abraham, Isaac, and Jacob.

Question 4

"What can we do about Christians who target us and our children?"

Standard Christian Answer:

The 'Jesus talk' begins. Christians generally view a question like this one as an opportunity to - what else?

Preach.

Seventeen Christian preachers visited Israel for the first time in February 2008. One pastor on the trip told a reporter: "The ultra-religious Jews take exception to Christianity, stating that 'the Nazis took the bodies of Jews but the Christians were trying to steal their souls.' They literally say that!" he exclaimed.

The statement made by an ultra-Orthodox Jew in Israel left the evangelical pastor from the United States astonished.

Sadly, he was astonished without reason. This pastor is an extraordinary and wonderful pro-Israel Christian man, but he was astonished because of his upside-down understanding of the comment. He was astonished because he had no reference point at all, for why a peace-loving, God-seeking man within the Jewish faith would say such a thing to a peace-loving, God-seeking man of the Christian faith.

But the heartfelt ultra-Orthodox response is not only a logically reasonable one: it is also nearly impossible for most Jews to think much differently.

Christendom has historically done all within its considerable influence to destroy Jews who will not convert, so any talk of conversion to that faith is very rationally perceived as an attempt to steal the souls of Jewish children.

> *For my Christian readers:*
> Religious Judaism, much like Christianity, has numerous denominations within their faith expression: Reform, Conservative, Modern Orthodox, Orthodox, ultra-Orthodox; each of these with varying theological differences and similarities. There are currently over 40,000 denominations within Christianity.

My pastor friend might be comforted by the fact that he has much company in his bewilderment. Many evangelicals don't know where to start in trying to understand the fearful, rage-filled statement of this Jewish father.

We should not be astonished that many Jews feel this way. We should be astonished and undone that the symbol of our cross has made them feel this way.

The Cross

"So I'll cherish the old rugged cross, till my trophies at last I lay down; I will cling to the old rugged cross and exchange it someday for a crown." (George Bennard, 1873-1958)

"The Old Rugged Cross," was one of the top ten most popular hymns of the twentieth century. For Christians, the cross is the iconic image of God's ultimate act of love. Christians believe it is the cross of Calvary where Jesus, as the Lamb of God, shed His blood and willingly gave up His life for the remission of mankind's sins.

Jews who have any acquaintance with the past two millennia of history also see the cross as a symbol of blood sacrifice. They see it from the experience of the apparently unquenchable Christian thirst for Jewish blood. They see it from the experience of proselytism by a historic Christian faith that apparently loves Jews only when they are on crosses. Thus, for many Jews, the cross is one of the most horrendous reminders of the 1,900 years of institutionalized Christian abominations that took place under its mandate.

The symbol of the cross has been seared into the history and flesh of the Jewish people.

Symbols Matter

Symbolic meanings can change, but not by decree. Only by real-time participation in a prolonged and renewed interactive experience with the symbol can the realities of it be changed.

Steve Jobs understood this to be true.

In the late 1960s and '70s, the Apple name and symbol meant only one thing: The Beatles. Apple Records was a division of the Beatles' tax haven of Apple Corp, founded in 1968. The label released all Beatles records after 1968 and also became the home to many other artists in the years that followed.

In 1977, Steve Jobs chose "Apple" as the brand name for his new computer company. And not since the time of Adam did a man have any less idea what he had just bitten into! Lawsuits with the Beatle's Apple Corp in 1978, 1986-1991, 2001, and 2007 cost Jobs tens of million of dollars.

But it was worth it. Symbols really matter, and symbols really can earn new meanings. Four long decades after the Beatles shook the world and left their musical and sociological mark in history, now, whenever someone speaks glowingly of "Apple," we don't immediately think of the Beatles. We know that person most likely speaks of an inordinately weird and deeply personal love relationship with all things Apple…

Apple Computers.

Likewise, the symbol of the old rugged cross solicits as much good will in the experience of the Jewish people as does the Nazi swastika, which for the Jews looks like a crooked cross.

To change the historic symbolic meaning of the cross as experienced and viewed by the Jewish community will not be as easy as the Apple metamorphosis Steve Jobs embarked upon. Changing a symbol of death and horror to one of life and hope will require a fundamental and sustainable change in Christian interaction with Jewish communities. It will first require an innate change within the heart of Christian faith and attitude toward the Jewish people.

I sincerely hope I do not offend my Jewish readers by using the comparison of such a trivial example to attempt to make a point about such a hideous one. If I have done so, please forgive me.

I only use this story because of its familiarity with my generation and with the hope of challenging prevalent Christian ignorance regarding contemporary Jewish rejection of our Christian "Good News" message. The regular e-mails I receive and conversations I have with many pro-Israel Christians who relay their dismay of "the Jew's hatred of Jesus" is alarming and painfully discouraging to me.

I cannot even start to imagine the turmoil a Jew experiences just by the reading of that false assumption.

Jews don't hate Jesus. Jews hate what has happened to them for so long, initiated by so many people who say they follow Jesus.

Conditioned by the Cross

Though conducted in the late 1890s, Dr. Pavlov's research in conditioning and involuntary reflex actions offers the Christian community insight into the horrendous desecration of the Jewish psyche caused by the Christian history's relentless tormenting of their people and faith.

In Dr. Pavlov's famous research, he introduced a study group (dogs) to a neutral object (a bell) and a significant object (dog food!) He started his experiment by ringing the bell every time he fed the dogs. Through the repetition of this procedure over an extended time, Pavlov discovered that ringing the bell alone (without the presentation of food) would cause the dogs to begin salivating. Pavlov called the dog's reaction to the bell a "conditioned response."

Why? Because they had been organically and psychologically conditioned into believing that every time they heard the ring of a bell the next thing they could expect was food.

The history of the church has conditioned the Jewish people.

I have heard many a Christian quote, "Fool me once, shame on you. Fool me twice, shame on me!" Consider for a moment our legacy of *fooling* the Jews.

Common sense alone would be more than sufficient reason for the Jewish community to give serious and long pause before offering the right hand of fellowship to Christians.

In addition to the rational trepidation of the Jewish community in regard to the newly proclaimed Christian love for them; the near-uninterrupted regularity with which they have been persecuted by the Christian societies they have lived in has also inflicted them with a self-preserving behavioral response to Christianity.

Due to our appalling failure to bless the Jewish people, the primary reason our preaching of the cross is repugnant to Jews is not because of what it means to us, but because of what we have made the cross mean to them.

Understanding the Passion

A Jewish friend recently added to my understanding concerning the Jews and our Passion of the Cross by sharing a very personal story about his mother. My dear friend, Hal Stein told me:

One day, many years ago, my sister and our cousin persuaded my late mother to respond to questions they asked about her life in 'the old country.' They taped the session.

My mother was born in 1902 in what is now known as the nation of Belarus, in a small village about eighty-five miles south of its capital, Minsk. At that time Belarus (Belorussia back then), bordering Poland, was a province of Russia. The population of my mother's old-world village was made up equally of Christians and Jews, and she grew up with friends of both faiths. One of the childhood experiences she painfully remembered in the taping

114

session related to an experience that took place almost every year on Good Friday.

As Easter approached, her Christian neighbor down the street would warn my grandmother that there was going to be trouble in the town. My grandmother would then pack up their bedding, lock up their house, and she and her three children would move in with the neighbor for the weekend. It wasn't safe for them to stay in their own home.

Following the Good Friday service, the Christian church-goers, mainly peasants who lived on farms in the outskirts, would stream out of their churches, having just heard a priestly tirade against 'the Jews who crucified Christ.' They would drink vodka and parade through the village, flaming with rage, ransacking and raiding Jewish-owned businesses. Any Jew foolish or unfortunate enough to be on the streets of the village during Good Friday would be attacked and struck down.

Listening to this particular memory of my mother's childhood, something became clear to me about certain memories of my own childhood in Sioux Falls, South Dakota.

I remembered long Sunday drives in the country with my parents. Going through town, whenever we passed a church where people were either entering or exiting, my mother would tense up and look straight ahead, sometimes muttering to herself. No doubt I must have sensed that her tension was related to seeing the churchgoers. We never talked about it, but it probably affected me, as I never wanted to have anything to do with churches, and I declined opportunities to join secular youth groups like Boy Scouts because they met in churches. No words were necessary for her son to understand at a very early age that there was some sort of inherent danger for Jews with churches...and with Christians.

The first realization of my lack of understanding concerning the Passion of the Cross from the Jewish point of view came into focus during the pre-promotion of the film "The Passion of the Christ." Like many Christians, I naively believed the uproar about this film from numerous Jewish community leaders was simply due to the fact that a movie about Jesus was coming out in major theaters around the nation.

"For crying out loud! Most of them hadn't even seen the thing yet and already they were complaining about it," I shamefully recall thinking.

At this point in my life, I just couldn't *feel* what the history of The Passion had meant to the Jews. Due to my complete ignorance concerning Christian/Jewish history, the Jewish leaders' cries for help sounded like whining to me-- and found no place of compassion or empathy in my heart.

Millions of Jews being burned at the stake and murdered was of course an abhorrent thought to me. But millions of lives cannot be emotionally fathomed, so they often become just a number with six zeros at the end of it unless one of those lives intimately touches yours.

And then, one night-- that is exactly what happened.

While at a pro-Israel planning meeting, one of our dearest and bravest of friends, a remarkable and remarkably beautiful seventy-year-old Jewish woman named Ruth, came into the living room where we all were gathered and quietly sat down. When this particular woman is sitting quietly, we all get worried! Without warning, Ruth suddenly burst into tears, and with apologetic sobs asked our forgiveness for her outburst.

"Ruthie," my wife whispered leaning toward our troubled friend. "What's wrong?"

Ruth tried to speak several times before she could actually continue.

"I am just so worried about this movie that is coming out," she wept. "Anti-Semitism is growing so quickly and to have another passion play being released around the world at this time is so dangerous to the Jews!" she explained to the room full of confused, dumb *goyim.*

For my Christian readers:

The word *goyim* means "nations" and refers to the fact that goyim are the members of nations, rather than the Children of Israel. Another term for a non-Jew is *Gentile.*

"And I am so worried about losing the Christian support!" Ruth continued with her fears.

"I'm kind of lost here, Ruth," I candidly confessed. "Why is the movie frightening to you and what does it have to do with Christian support?" I asked, realizing just how lost I really was.

Ruth then read an article to us that described how Ted Haggard, the President of the National Association of Evangelicals, warned Jews that lobbying against the film could cost them evangelical support for Israel.

There is a great deal of pressure on Israel right now, and Christians seem to be a major source of support for Israel. For the Jewish leaders to risk alienating two billion Christians over a movie might seem short-sighted. But to suggest that Christian support for the Jewish people is so fickle as to be contingent upon their enjoying the same movies as we do seems more than a little shortsighted-- and frighteningly shallow.

Honestly, until that evening, most of us had never heard of Ted Haggard, but we were livid at his remarks. He heard from all of us by the next day, as we each contacted his office with our rage over his dimwitted and mean-spirited remarks concerning Christian support for the Jews.

The room was absolutely silent except for the muffled crying of our dear Ruthie. And then my wife spoke – and asked all of our Jewish friends in the room to forgive us for the sins committed throughout our horrid history with them.

It was the first time in my life I had ever heard a Christian ask a Jew for forgiveness.

My wife's words pierced me with their guilty righteousness and I followed in her holy example, asking for their forgiveness as well.

Our gracious Jewish friends quickly attempted to dissuade us from any sense of historic culpability – but it was too late for that.

We had just felt and seen the terrible scarring our history had left upon a real, live Jew for whom we really did care. The wounds of our friend had wounded our hearts as well, and finally, after twenty years of pro-Israel activism we were beginning to really love the Jews.

I came across a newspaper article by Marvin Hier and Harold Brackman about Mel Gibson's as-yet-unreleased film "The Passion of the Christ":

Cecil B. DeMille's 1927 biblical epic "The King of Kings" offended American Jews by portraying the Jewish people-- rather than the Romans-- as responsible for the crucifixion of Jesus. DeMille dismissed criticism, insisting that, "if Jesus were alive today, these Jews I speak of might crucify him again."

But whether DeMille admitted it or not, the film did fuel anti-Semitism....

Now comes Mel Gibson, who insists Jews and Catholics will have nothing to worry about in his new, self-financed, $25-million film, "The Passion." It's true that the final script hasn't been made available, and there is currently no release date, or even distributor, for the film. Still, there are reasons for concern.

The passion of Christ-- the crucifixion and hours leading up to it-- has been used by bigots, including popes and kings, to inflame anti-Semitism through the ages. A belief that Jews were responsible for crucifying the son of God led Pope Innocent III to conclude in the early 13th century that Jews should be consigned to a state of "perpetual subservience" as wanderers and fugitives, and made to wear a mark on their clothing identifying them as Jews. His pronouncement reinforced widespread anti-Semitism that led over the centuries to millions of Jews being burned at the stake and murdered in pogroms throughout Christian Europe.

Any film about such a sensitive subject would set off alarm bells.... Gibson should consider the political context before bringing out his film. Globally, anti-Semitism is at its highest peak since the end of World War II. Synagogues and Jewish schools have been firebombed and Jews beaten on the streets of France and Belgium. According to some recent polls, 17% of Americans (up from 12% five years ago) hold to political and economic stereotypes about Jews; 37% hold Jews responsible for the death of Jesus. At this tinderbox moment in our new century, we need to be especially careful about a movie that has the potential to further ignite ancient hatreds.

Pure, Genuine-- and Rare-- Christian Religion

Some Christian readers are possibly pursing their lips and swaying their heads in condemnation as they smugly dismiss my psychological theorizing and ecumenical love for the Jews. I can see angry verses flying my way. "But the Bible says this, and the Bible says that about the Jews!"

I'm familiar with the Book.

And I am aware the Bible says many things about many things. Simply reciting verses in the direction of those we've sinned against is not one of the practices the New Testament encourages or condones.

James 1:27

If you claim to be religious but don't control your tongue, you are fooling yourself, and your religion is worthless.

The authenticity of our faith is not only found in the words we speak – but also in those we do not speak.

But the ultimate expression of the Christian faith is evidenced through our actions toward others.

Ephesians 2:10

For we are God's handiwork, created in Christ Jesus to do good works, which God prepared in advance for us to do.

James 1:27

Pure and genuine religion in the sight of God the Father means caring for orphans and widows in their distress and refusing to let the world corrupt you.

Tragically, Jewish people have never received much genuine religion from our camp.

The Practice of Target Practice

Especially disconcerting to the Jewish community are Christians who claim love for the Jews, yet continue to treat them like nothing more than conversion targets-- confirming exactly what many Jews feel they represent to us.

Since the Jews have been the primary recipients of Christian depravity and hatred almost from the birth of our faith, one would think that Christians could grasp why a "Jesus tract" slipped under the windshield or shoved into the hand of a Jew is so repugnant to them. Before confronting Jews with the enormity of love we claim to have for them, shouldn't every Christian at least say something like, "Hey... sure sorry about hunting down and persecuting you guys for so long!"

In the last few years, there have been numerous well-meaning announcements made from Christian denominations along with (very expensive) full-page ads in major newspapers proclaiming *the Jews* need of salvation. The declarations usually include a full court press for evangelizing Jews with the Gospel message. The notices are usually laced with sentiments of "great love and respect" for the Jews, along with New Testament Bible verses.

These types of publications must swirl the DNA and memories of the Jewish people with grim reminders of being targeted with our Gospel message throughout history.

I'm sure they find it frighteningly reminiscent of our short-lived Martin Luther chapter of great love and respect for the Jews.

I'm sure they also wonder how long this current episode of Christian love for them will last-- if they don't convert.

For the Jew, history does have a way of repeating itself.

The next time any Christians really feel a need to target a specific group of people in *The New York Times*, why not just put together a full-page ad like this:

THE GOSPEL AND THE MUSLIM PEOPLE
AN EVANGELICAL STATEMENT

We of the Christian faith want to express our genuine love for the Muslims of the world, but at the same time make known our belief that the threat of militant Islam is a grave danger to the existence of Israel and the entire world.

~ We now deplore the killing people in the name of God.

~ We of the Christian faith therefore now announce that because of our love and profound respect for Muslims, we must remind them that it is only through faith in Jesus Christ that they can receive eternal life.

~ We call upon Christians everywhere to help us share our faith with Muslims in this Crusade of Love!

We want to make it clear that, as evangelical Christians, we do not wish to offend our Muslim friends by the above statements, but we are compelled by our convictions to the Holy Scriptures. It is out of our profound respect for Muslims that we seek to share the good news of Jesus Christ with them, and encourage others to do the same, for we believe that salvation is only found in Jesus, the Savior of the world.

We really, really, <u>really</u> hope and pray that none of the above statements have offended any Muslims, anywhere.

The sponsors of this ad would rather not have their names published.

Why don't we ever see Christians running ads like that?

Why don't we see Christians running ads that would target the lost Scientologists of Hollywood. Why don't Christians target all the lost workaholic attorneys of New York or the lost and out-of-work realtors and mortgage lenders of the nation or...? But most of all, why *do* Christians target the Jews-- and call it loving and respecting the Jews?

Answering the question:
"What can we do about Christians who target us and our children?"

I suggest every Christian take the time necessary to make some close Jewish friends. Real friendships can't happen overnight so you'll really need to be committed to loving the Jews, if you are going to have the actual experience of loving a Jew. After you have laughed and wept together, attended synagogue and eaten many meals together, worked against anti-Semitism and for the continued security of the nation of Israel together-- *then* ask your Jewish friend if Jews feel loved by us-- when they feel targeted by us.

I was once part of a panel discussion at an AIPAC Conference in Washington, DC. During the Q & A, a young Jewish college student shared the following familiar story:

"Christian groups on our campus often approach us and say they want to work with us," she stated with a sigh. "The problem is, they are so aggressive with their evangelizing, we all feel as though we are just 'targets' to them," she cautiously continued, wondering if she should be ashamed of her honest confession.

"We appreciate all the help we can get, but what can we say to them to get them to just, you know-- help us?" she finished in an almost apologetic tone.

I asked forgiveness on behalf of my Christian faith for the impious chafing this Daughter of Zion had endured on her campus. I told her the crux of the Christian faith was to make people feel loved by us, not hunted by us. I paused before answering her question, trying (with little success) to temper my response, "You know what you can do about it?

"Tell the Christians who can't stop preaching about Jesus-- to please stop." I stood in her defense. (At this point, I thought I heard squeaking from a chair in the direction of another pastor on the stage, trying to quietly sneak away from me!)

"Tell those Christians preaching at you that if they really do want to work with you to stop talking and start doing!

"Remind them that the nation of Israel and the Jewish people are facing very real, grave, and present dangers and you welcome their friendship. Tell them to live exemplary lives as they walk with you, and that if you ever have any questions about why they believe and behave as they do-- you will ask them!

"Tell them that," I reiterated.

I then finished, "If they really do love you they will probably thank you for your honesty, roll up their sleeves and get to work! Hopefully they will become trusted friends and demonstrate lives of true Biblical Christian love."

Amen to that hope.
It is what we were created, in Jesus Christ - to do.

Ephesians 2:10

For we are God's workmanship, created in Christ Jesus to do good works, which God prepared in advance for us to do.

Rabbi Yossi and Rabbi Mendy
Two very dear friends who have changed my life.

Question 5
"Why don't you educate the anti-Israel churches?"

Standard Christian Answer:
"Are there churches that are really against Israel?"
And believe it or not - the "Jesus talk" begins.

Throwing Kisses and Beating Up Bishops

I received a phone call from a fellow Christian supporter of Israel, inviting me to an evening debate concerning peace in the Middle East. One of Sacramento's most liberal churches was hosting the discussion. The event was open to the general public, and two members of the Jewish community from the university town of Davis would be available to answer questions.

The presentation purported to offer a balanced approach, in contrast to a decidedly anti-Israel stance the church had previously sponsored. Aware of the reputation and theology of the congregation, we anticipated this follow-up evening would offer anything but an unprejudiced view.

An added incentive for attending the event was the word that Walid Shoebat was in town. This former Palestinian terrorist, now a confirmed pro-Israel Christian, would be joining us at the brawl-- uh, church meeting.

For my Christian readers:

As a young man, Walid Shoebat became a member of the Palestinian Liberation Organization. He participated in acts of terror and violence against Israel and was later imprisoned in the Russian Compound, Jerusalem's central prison for incitement and violence against Israel. After his release, he continued his life of violence and rioting in Bethlehem and at the Temple Mount. After entering the U.S., he worked as a counselor for the Arab Student Organization at Loop College in Chicago, continuing his anti-Israel activities.

In 1993, Walid studied the Old Testament as a challenge to convert his wife to Islam. After six months of intense study, Walid realized that everything he had been taught about Jews was a lie. Convinced that he had been operating on the side of evil, he chose to become an advocate for his former enemy, the Jews.

Go to: www.shoebat.com for more information.

I made some phone invitations to likeminded associates to strengthen our cause. A few hours later, we all met in the Episcopal Church lobby for the event. As we made introductions of Walid and ourselves to the bishop who would be running the show, we seemed to feel the temperature around us drop about thirty degrees and we sensed that the evening would bring a head-on clash with our liberal Christian brothers.

The bishop's opening ceremony was not a prayer. Rather, he pontificated about Israel's "historic and continued acts of hostility" against the Palestinian people. His solemn vapors filled the room and were quickly fanned into a flame by a man in the front row who identified himself as a Jew. This man did not mention in his self-introduction that he was also a hater of Israeli Jews, although his feelings were soon made evident by his spoken condemnations pertaining to every aspect of the nation of Israel.

Every hand from our group shot up into the air to answer this self-absorbed Jewish anti-Semite. He was allowed to drone on, uninterrupted. The bishop nodded his head in agreement with the profoundly inaccurate accusations made by his front-row advocate as we continued to wave our hands in the air like elementary school children in desperate need of a potty break.

The bishop seemed to find in the audience only those with their hands politely raised. As he called on them, each echoed, not surprisingly, the sentiments of the teacher's pet in the front row.

And so the evening went.

At one point, Walid was finally acknowledged. As he began speaking, his words displayed the authority of the only person in the room who had actually been raised in the Middle East. As he made the argument for Israel's many amazing humanitarian efforts for its Palestinian citizens, Walid was quickly cut off. Another attendee with the "appropriate" perspective was given permission to talk.

The Jewish guests from Davis, California – marched to the front of the room like sheep to the slaughter and were immediately assaulted with angry statements rather than questions from an audience that grew more spiteful by the minute.

As the couple bravely stood their ground behind a wobbly wooden pulpit set in front of them, the reverend made a power move so grievous that our entire side of the room groaned out loud! For the third time in a row, he called upon his Jew-hating front row companion to make yet another comment-- and I lost it.

Standing up, I yelled, "You can't do that!" as our entire gang of Christian Zionists (plus a couple of Jewish buddies with us) jumped up and started shouting about the injustice of the entire evening. Before we could get kicked out, we slowly walked out of the lecture hall, continuing our rowdy protest.

I threw kisses to the Jewish couple at the front of the hall and cried out, "We love you! We love you! These guys don't represent us: you have many, many Christian friends!"

The two guests from Davis smiled as we marched out the door in our angry parade. They beamed at our passionate outburst, and-- I believe-- at our professed love for them as well.

For the record: this is not how we usually conduct ourselves, nor is it how we train others to interact with the detractors of Israel. But it sure felt good making such a fuss in that corrupt environment.

We regrouped in the garden area outside the social hall while the dishonest "debate" continued inside. A few others who apparently agreed with our uprising followed our lead and slowly trickled out of the church social hall. With them came the junior bishop of the cathedral, who had been assigned the task of asking us to leave their property. I was actually comforted when he referred to the facility as "their" property, seeing that it certainly did not represent a true house of worship.

I had just finished cooling a heated conversation between a person from our group and a representative from the church who had followed us outside when I heard Walid warn the junior bishop, "Touch me again-- go ahead, touch me again and see what happens!"

Frantically zigzagging through the small crowd that was calmly discussing the events of the evening, I grabbed Walid and, wrapping my arms around his considerable shoulders, announced, "Come on, Brother; we're done here."

He tried to shake himself free from my restraint as he continued urging the young bishop to "touch me one more time." I whispered a Hebrew proverb in his ear, "Do not answer a fool in his folly lest you become like him," and cautioned, "It's already happened, brother; let's get out of here!"

Without waiting for his approval, I pushed and pulled with all of my strength, inching him off the church property. I suddenly felt the resistance in his body slough to the ground as he resigned himself to my unsolicited intervention. I released my death grip, and we walked together toward the peaceful (and sane) buffer zone of the city-owned sidewalks of Sacramento.

My dear wife, who had been in the thick of the entire episode, was the first one to speak after we silently re-gathered our troops, our thoughts, and our dignity: "There sure is a lot of testosterone here right now!" she laughed out loud. Yep, there sure was.

The Problem with Educating Anti-Semitic Christians

The entirety of the Hebrew proverb that I recited to my friend Walid is as follows:

Proverbs 26:4-5

Answer not a fool according to his folly, lest thou also be like unto him. Answer a fool according to his folly, lest he be wise in his own eyes.

In other words, there is a time to walk away from those who are expounding foolishness and there is a time to confront them. Hopefully, through our attempts to know the Almighty and recognize His voice, we can be divinely guided through these types of disagreements.

In the story I just shared, none of us were looking all that attentively for guidance from our Maker. That night, however, became a memorial of sorts for our pro-Israel efforts. We did learn a critical truth through the chaos we experienced and the ensuing fireworks that we lit.

We recognized-- not for the first time-- that there are folks in this world, including Christian folks, who do not reference the same compass as we do. Our north is their south; some things we call righteous, they deem wicked and vice versa. There certainly is opportunity for differences of opinions in our debates, including all topics. There is room for criticizing Israel when she has behaved in away that is unworthy of her stature as a nation. With that said, however, the pseudo-debates demonizing every action of the nation of Israel do not fall within the category of "difference of opinion." Most of the anti-Israel rhetoric being printed and spoken around the world is actually Jewish hatred, and anti-Semitism in any form is a dark and wicked sin, damning the soul of man. Clothing the prejudice in political or religious argument neither softens it nor makes the adherence to it any less detestable to the Almighty.

Isaiah 5:20

Woe unto them that call evil good, and good evil; that change darkness into light, and light into darkness; that change bitter into sweet, and sweet into bitter!

Matthew 6:22-23

Your eye is a lamp that provides light for your body.
When your eye is good, your whole body is filled with light.
But when your eye is bad, your whole body is filled with darkness.
And if the light you think you have is actually darkness, how deep
that darkness is!

Educating the Educable

As Christian Zionists, we have made the decision to invest the best of our time, strength, and efforts in events where we can educate those people most inclined to support the nation of Israel. We refer to this strategy as "reaching the low-hanging fruit." In the Christian community, reaching, teaching and engaging evangelicals has become our primary goal.

Martin Luther employed the word *evangelical* to identify a specific doctrinal tradition, defining those Christians who left the Roman Catholic Church. The word *evangelical* came from an ancient Greek term for "good news," and it meant both the good news of Jesus Christ and the good news regarding the faith of a people who believed they were created to help heal the hurting of mankind. William Wilberforce used the word to describe his faith while fighting British slavery.

As noted in Chapter 1, Luther strayed far from his own early convictions regarding the Scriptures' clear and constant heralding of God's everlasting love for the Jewish people.

For my Christian readers:

As a reminder I include more of Luther's thoughts concerning the Jews from his diatribe "On the Jews and Their Lies":

"They [rulers] must act like a good physician who, when gangrene has set in, proceeds without mercy to cut, saw, and burn

133

flesh, veins, bone, and marrow. Such a procedure must also be followed in this instance. Burn down their synagogues, forbid all that I enumerated earlier, force them to work, and deal harshly with them, as Moses did . . . If this does not help we must drive them out like mad dogs." --Martin Luther, 1543

It is not simply because evangelicals read the Bible that we are passionate supporters of the Jewish people: it is *the way we read it* that births a love for Jews within our hearts. The evangelical creed believes in the authority of the Bible as being "God-breathed" or inspired by God, and to be read and understood as such. Because of this core belief, the pro-Israel education of evangelical Christians begins in the study of the Hebrew and Greek scriptures. What an amazing moment when, during the course of such studies, you see the lights go on inside the hearts and minds of the congregation!

Once an individual has his Biblical paradigm established concerning the Jewish people and the land of Israel, that belief is secured within his or her personal convictions and is near unchangeable. Evangelicals teach that the Bible is to be interpreted through the same rules followed in everyday conversation.

"When the plain sense of Scripture makes common sense, seek no other sense; therefore, take every word at its primary, ordinary, usual, literal meaning unless the facts of the immediate context, studied in the light of related passages and axiomatic and fundamental truths, indicate clearly otherwise." --Dr. David L. Cooper, the late founder and director of the Biblical Research Society.

For instance, if in the course of a discussion a person tells you a dream he had, you interpret his comments by first understanding he is talking to you about a dream. You comprehend immediately as he relates specifics that he did not actually "eat a two-story-tall marshmallow," but that this was a scene of his dream. In addition, the dream may appear to have specific meaning-- or may only be the after-effects of a late-night burrito snack.

Judges 7:13

And when Gideon was come, behold, there was a man telling a dream unto his fellow, and saying: "Behold, I dreamed a dream, and, lo, a cake of barley bread tumbled into the camp of Midian, and came unto the tent, and smote it that it fell, and turned it upside down, that the tent lay flat."

Evangelicals interpret this portion of Scripture with the understanding that the story is about a dream; i.e., there was not a literal loaf of barley bread that tumbled into a campground and smashed somebody's tent. Neither is this portion of scripture to be taken as a metaphor concerning the trials of life or the dangers of cooking outdoors. It simply is what it is: a dream. This particular dream is then interpreted for us:

Judges 7:14

And his fellow answered and said: "This is nothing else save the sword of Gideon the son of Joash, a man of Israel: into his hand God hath delivered Midian, and all the host."

We are then told that Gideon, eavesdropping on the entire exchange, takes the dream and interpretation as a sign from God, goes back to his camp, and gets his guys ready to rumble.

Judges 7:15

And it was so, when Gideon heard the telling of the dream, and the interpretation thereof, that he worshipped; and he returned into the camp of Israel, and said: "Arise; for God hath delivered into your hand the host of Midian."

In the most basic of guidelines, this process delineates how true evangelicals read the Torah, the Prophets, the Writings, and the Greek scriptures as well.

For my Christian readers:

Judaism refers to the first five books of the Hebrew Bible as the Torah. (Your Jewish friends will appreciate it if you do not call their scriptures the Old Testament). There are three sections to the Hebrew Bible or, as it is called in Hebrew, the TaNaKH: an acronym for Torah, Prophets, and Writings. Torah means "teaching" and is God's revealed instructions to the Jewish people. It was given to the children of Israel at Mount Sinai during their exodus from Egypt approximately 3,500 years ago. The Prophets are direct prophecies or recordings of what was said to the prophets, and the Writings are books written by the prophets with the guidance of God.

Evangelical Christians read and understand the parables of Jesus as teaching illustrations. The book of Proverbs is a book of observed wisdom and not a book of promises to us. We read and understand the Hebrew books of poetry-- the Psalms, the Song of Solomon, etc.-- as poetry, written with the divine use of parallelisms.

We know, since the Bible uses anthropomorphic metaphors for the Almighty, such as in Psalm 18, that God does not have a nose!

Psalm 18:15

The valleys of the sea were exposed and the foundations of the earth laid bare at your rebuke, O Lord, at the blast of breath from your nostrils.

Christians are supposed to recognize that even in the best of our Biblical conclusions, we see and understand the person of God through a hazy and finite view:

Corinthians 13:11-13

When I was a child, I spoke and thought and reasoned as a child. But when I grew up, I put away childish things. Now we see things imperfectly as in a cloudy mirror, but then we will see everything with perfect clarity. All that I know now is partial and incomplete, but then I will know everything completely, just as God now knows me completely. Three things will last forever-- faith, hope, and love-- and the greatest of these is love.

How unspeakably tragic that Christianity does not have a legacy of faith, hope, and love-- toward the Jewish people.

How to Identify Pro-Israel Evangelicals

How can you distinguish pro-Israel evangelicals from the others who use the same literal interpretation of the Scriptures? Evangelicals who read the following verse from Jonah simply believe that God told a great fish to swallow His hesitant prophet and then commanded the fish to hold him captive in its belly for three days and three nights. We might disagree over the type of fish, but we will not argue over the clear narrative describing one very large creature and its swallowing of Jonah.

Jonah 1:17

And God appointed a great fish to swallow Jonah, and Jonah was in the stomach of the fish three days and three nights.

Some argue, "How could such a thing happen?"

Evangelicals read these things and say, "With God, all things are possible"

137

So when we evangelicals muse over the myriad verses in the Torah that speak of God's everlasting covenants and love for the Jewish people, we simply believe the verses are absolute and indisputable truths.

Genesis 5 17:7

I will establish My covenant between Me and you and your descendants after you throughout their generations for an everlasting covenant, to be God to you and to your descendants after you.

1 Kings 10:9

Blessed be HaShem your God Who delighted in you to set you on the throne of Israel; because HaShem loved Israel forever.

Isaiah 49:14-16

But Zion said, "God has forsaken me, God has forgotten me."
"Can a mother forget the baby at her breast and have no compassion on the child she has borne? Though she may forget, I will not forget you! See, I have engraved you on the palms of my hands; your walls are ever before me."

We believe the Jewish prophets foretold the worldwide Diaspora of the Jewish people, after which God one day would bring them back to the land He had given them.

Jeremiah 16:14-15

"Therefore, behold, the days are coming," says the Lord, "when it shall no more be said, 'As the Lord lives, Who brought up the children of Israel out of the land of Egypt'; But the days are coming when it will be said...'As the Lord lives, Who brought up the children of Israel from the land of the north and from all the countries to which they have been scattered.' For I will bring them again to their land which I gave to their fathers."

Ezekiel 34:11-13

For this is what the Sovereign Lord says: "I myself will search for my sheep and look after them. As a shepherd looks after his scattered flock when he is with them, so will I look after my sheep. I will rescue them from all the places where they were scattered on a day of clouds and darkness. I will bring them out from the nations and gather them from the countries, and I will bring them into their own land."

Pro-Israel evangelicals also take to heart the many New Testament verses that remind us of the unique place in the Almighty's heart for His firstborn, the Jewish people:

Romans 9:4-5

Theirs [the Jewish people's] is the adoption as sons; theirs the divine glory, the covenants, the receiving of the law, the temple worship and the promises. Theirs are the patriarchs, and from them is traced the human ancestry of Christ....

Matthew 15:22-28

A Canaanite [Gentile] woman from that vicinity came to him, crying out, "Lord, Son of David, have mercy on me! My daughter is suffering terribly from demon-possession."

Jesus did not answer a word. So his disciples came to him and urged him, "Send her away, for she keeps crying out after us."

He answered, "I was sent only to the lost sheep of Israel."

The woman came and knelt before him. "Lord, help me!" she said.

He replied, "It is not right to take the children's bread and toss it to the dogs."

"Yes, Lord," she said, "but even the dogs eat the crumbs that fall from their master's table."

Then Jesus answered, "Woman, you have great faith! Your request is granted." And her daughter was healed from that very hour.

The dogs, huh?
OK, that's pretty clear.

For evangelicals, it is obvious in the Scriptures that the Jewish people were and are God's first love. Also obvious to us is that God has a continuing relationship with the Jewish people and a uniquely glorious destiny for them.

Romans 11:1

I ask then: "Has God rejected his own people, the nation of Israel? God forbid-- may it never be so!"

Romans 11:11

I say then, "Did they stumble that they might fall? God forbid-- may it never be so!"

Through this form of interpretation of the Bible, we establish our convictions about every aspect of our Christian faith.

Many within the non-evangelical Christian community see the Bible as inspired by man and riddled with inconsistencies. In so doing, they tend to embrace a nonliteral and politically liberal view of the Scriptures and thus have a liberal spirituality and worldview. This variety of theology generally excludes the unique and enormous significance that evangelicals see placed by the Almighty upon the nation of Israel, the Jewish people and His promises to them.

The "Other" Evangelicals

A few days after our very successful 2007 Christians United For Israel, Israel/D.C. Summit, President George W. Bush received the following letter from a group of men identifying themselves as evangelical leaders in the United States.

Letter to President Bush from Evangelical Leaders
President George W. Bush
The White House
1600 Pennsylvania Ave NW
Washington DC 20500

Dear Mr. President:

We write as evangelical Christian leaders in the United States to thank you for your efforts (including the major address on July 16) to reinvigorate the Israeli-Palestinian negotiations to achieve a lasting peace in the region. We affirm your clear call for a two-state solution. We urge that your administration not grow weary in the time it has left in office to utilize the vast influence of America to demonstrate creative, consistent and determined U.S. leadership to create a new future for Israelis and Palestinians. We pray to that end, Mr. President.

We also write to correct a serious misperception among some people, including some U.S. policymakers, that all American evangelicals are opposed to a two-state solution and creation of a new Palestinian state that includes the vast majority of the West Bank. Nothing could be further from the truth. We who sign this letter, represent large numbers of evangelicals throughout the U.S. who support justice for both Israelis and Palestinians. We hope this support will embolden you and your administration to proceed confidently and forthrightly in negotiations with both sides in the region.

As evangelical Christians, we embrace the biblical promise to Abraham: "I will bless those who bless you." (Genesis 12:3). And precisely as evangelical Christians committed to the full teaching of the Scriptures, we know that blessing and loving people (including Jews and the present State of Israel) does not mean withholding criticism when it is warranted. Genuine love and genuine blessing means acting in ways that promote the genuine and long-term wellbeing of our neighbors. Perhaps the best way we can bless Israel is to encourage her to remember, as she deals with her neighbor Palestinians, the profound teaching on justice that the Hebrew prophets proclaimed so forcefully as an inestimably precious gift to the whole world. Historical honesty compels us to recognize that both Israelis and Palestinians have legitimate rights

---

stretching back for millennia to the lands of Israel/Palestine. Both Israelis and Palestinians have committed violence and injustice against each other. The only way to bring the tragic cycle of violence to an end is for Israelis and Palestinians to negotiate a just, lasting agreement that guarantees both sides viable, independent, secure states. To achieve that goal, both sides must give up some of their competing, incompatible claims. Israelis and Palestinians must both accept each other's right to exist. And to achieve that goal, the U.S. must provide robust leadership within the Quartet to reconstitute the Middle East roadmap, whose full implementation would guarantee the security of the State of Israel and the viability of a Palestinian State. We affirm the new role of former Prime Minister Tony Blair and pray that the conference you plan for this fall will be a success.

Mr. President, we renew our prayers and support for your leadership to help bring peace to Jerusalem, and justice and peace for all the people in the Holy Land.

Finally, we would request to meet with you to personally convey our support and discuss other ways in which we may help your administration on this crucial issue.

Sincerely,
Ronald J. Sider, President Evangelicals for Social Action

(And 29 others – too much space would be taken to list the names.)

No surprise: On July 29, 2007, *The New York Times* published the entire letter.

Now that I have reread the letter since its publication, I am again mystified by the intellectual and theological dishonesty of its contents. Any discussion that includes the phrase "the tragic cycle of violence" concerning the turmoil between the nation of Israel and the Palestinian people or surrounding Arab nations is disqualified from being taken seriously. Israel wants peace with her 22 primarily Arab/Muslim neighbor nations. Not one of the 22 nations surrounding Israel will recognize her right to exist as the homeland of the Jewish people. Peace will come to the Middle

142

East 10 minutes after these nations lay their guns down and embrace the right of their Jewish stepbrothers to exist in the land of Israel.

[Please see page 157: "MESSAGE FROM DAVID BROG," CUFI EXECUTIVE DIRECTOR.]

The "other" Evangelical leaders suggest that they alone represent the Christian community that is in favor of "justice" in the Middle East conflict. The important question we first need answered is, "Whose concept of justice are we going to use as our standard?"

If I give my daughter a bike for her birthday and someone wants to take it from her, is there justice in allowing the one who wants her bike to take it? If we are using my standard of justice as a father, and as the giver of the gift, then I say my daughter is justified in her rights to keep her bike. The person who would like to have the bike can disagree with me. He can even try to make a case as to why he needs the bike, but in this case, I am not inclined to adopt his standard of justice should he repeatedly try to take it from her.

Now should my daughter choose to share, or even give the bike to another, that is absolutely her prerogative. When pro-Israel evangelicals speak of justice concerning the Jewish people and the land of Israel, we start with the conviction that *this bike was promised* to the descendants of Abraham, Isaac, and Jacob.

Genesis 13:14-15

God said to Abram, after Lot had separated from him, "Now lift up your eyes and look from the place where you are, northward and southward and eastward and westward; for all the land which you see, I will give it to you and to your descendants forever."

Genesis 15:18-21

On that day God made a covenant with Abram, saying, "To your descendants I have given this land, from the river of Egypt as far as the great river, the river Euphrates: the Kenite and the Kenizzite and the Kadmonite and the Hittite and the Perizzite and the Rephaim and the Amorite and the Canaanite and the Girgashite and the Jebusite."

Genesis 28:12-14

And behold, God stood above it and said, "I am the God of your father Abraham and the God of Isaac; the land on which you lie, I will give it to you and to your descendants."

Exodus 6:8

And I will bring you to the land I swore with uplifted hand to give to Abraham, to Isaac and to Jacob. I will give it to you as a possession. I am the Lord.

There are many, many verses that reiterate this promise to the descendants of Abraham, Isaac, and Jacob. Unfortunately, you can call yourself an evangelical and select the verses that are immutable and then select those verses where you perceive God meant something opposite of what He said. And to be honest, many Christians do use selective verse theology to gratify their own philosophical and sociological leanings and to empower the preaching of their own prejudices.

The evangelicals who wrote the above letter to President Bush present an excellent example of religious bias as they claim to embrace the biblical promise to Abraham: *"I will bless those who bless you-- "*

Such an odd place they chose to end the quote-- right in the middle of the sentence! Is it absentmindedness or convenience that they omit the totality of the promise of Genesis?

Genesis 12:3

*"I will bless those who bless you **and curse those who curse you.**"*

Their omitted section of the second portion of this covenant undeniably changes *the profound teaching on justice* so forcefully proclaimed by the Hebrew prophets. Their anti-Israel perspective is primarily formed from a liberal worldview where the strong oppress the weak. When it comes to the Arab/Israeli Conflict, they view Israel as having strength, making her the oppressor. The Palestinians are viewed as being weak, and are therefore the oppressed.

These Christians have allowed their liberal worldview to form their un-Biblical theological view and it forces them to ignore the God-given eternal land grant of Canaan into the hands of the descendants of Abraham, Isaac and Jacob.

Part of their spiritual definition of justice is attributed to their secular definition of oppression. It is a desire to "free the oppressed," thus bringing *justice* to the region that explains their opinions of, and solutions to the Israeli/Palestinian conflict. Their attempts to robe and validate their views in Christian theology do not change the sinfulness of them.

Their anti-Israel theology and liberal worldview force them to rewrite history. I would sure love to see their resources regarding this statement from their letter to the President:

"Historical honesty compels us to recognize that both Israelis and Palestinians have legitimate rights stretching back for millennia to the lands of Israel/Palestine."

This is historical *dishonesty* that is beyond understanding.

For my Christian readers:

In the 2nd century C.E., the Roman emperor Hadrian renamed the land of Judah *Palestine*, after the extinct people and enemies of Israel, the Philistines. In recent history, the term "Palestinian" was viewed by Arabs living in Palestine as a derogatory colonialist British term, designed to erase their Arab identity. The Arabs living in Palestine never had a separate state and simply saw themselves as part of the larger Arab or Muslim community. It was Yasser Arafat who began using the term *Palestinian* in 1964 to describe the Arabs living in Israel and their national identity.

"There is no such country as Palestine. "Palestine" is a term the Zionists invented. There is no Palestine in the Bible. Our country was, for centuries, part of Syria. Palestine is alien to us. It is the Zionists who introduced it." --Auni Bey Abdul-Hadi, Syrian Arab leader to British Peel Commission, 1937

The Palestine Symphony

Until the early 1950's, the term Palestinian was used in reference to the Jews living in Israel. The Palestine Symphony Orchestra was founded in 1936 as conditions in Europe had become such that the orchestra served as a haven for persecuted Jewish musicians. Many immigration certificates became available, as the orchestra could provide employment for the refugees.

146

The Palestine Post

The Palestine Post was the Jewish-owned and -operated English-language daily established in Jerusalem in 1932 as part of a Zionist-Jewish initiative. In 1950 its name was changed to *The Jerusalem Post* and it continues to be published under that name to this day.

The Palestine Potash Company

In 1930, a major industry was launched on the barren shores of the Dead Sea, the Palestine Potash Company. Established by Moshe Novomeysky, the company was responsible for almost half the worth of all of the exports of the Jews of Palestine by 1940.

The Promises of God

Pro-Israel evangelicals differentiate between the Conditional Covenants and the Unconditional Covenants (promises) God has made with the Jewish people. The Conditional Covenants of God are understood through the prescribed agreement of "*If* you do such and such, *then* I will OR *will not* do so and so."

An Unconditional Covenant is also defined as a unilateral covenant: "I will do such and such!" It is a promise or series of promises that God has made with the Jewish people whereby He *unconditionally* obligates Himself to bring to pass definite promises made to His covenanted people. These promises are guaranteed to be fulfilled based exclusively upon the intentions and integrity of the one making the promise-- in this case, Almighty God! The inheritance of Canaan, the land of Israel, is noted as an Unconditional Covenant.

Genesis 13:15

"Now lift up your eyes and look from the place where you are, northward and southward and eastward and westward; for all the

land which you see, I will give it to you and to your descendants forever."

Though the inheritance of the Land of Israel was an Unconditional Covenant, possessing the Land of Israel had conditions:

II Kings 21:8

If the Israelites will be careful to obey my commands—all the laws my servant Moses gave them, I will not send them into exile from this land that I gave their ancestors.

The Children of Israel did *not* live according to the Law of Moses and God kept His promise, exiling them from the Land of their inheritance. The Babylonian exile of the Jews is both historically and Biblically recorded, as is the second exile of 70 AD by the Romans.

Ezekiel 36:17.19

"Son of man, when the people of Israel were living in their own land, they defiled it by the evil way they lived.

I scattered them to many lands to punish them for the evil way they had lived."

Matthew 24

As Jesus was leaving the Temple grounds, his disciples pointed out to him the various Temple buildings. But he responded, "Do you see all these buildings? I tell you the truth, they will be completely demolished. Not one stone will be left on top of another!"

But their possession of the land (living in the land) and their inheritance of the land (ownership of the land) are two different types of covenants-- and it is our generation that has witnessed God's faithfulness to His promises, in returning the descendants of Abraham, Isaac, and Jacob to once again possess the land of Israel!

Amillennialism and Replacement Theology

Certain Christian theological views make the notion of Jews having any enduring covenant with the Almighty (apart from faith in Jesus Christ) a sacrilegious thought. Amillennialists believe that the as-yet-unfulfilled Biblical covenants God made with the Children of Israel are either fulfilled spiritually in The Church, or that the promises made to the Jewish people need not be fulfilled at all.

Replacement theology (also known as Supersessionism) teaches that because the Jews did not recognize Jesus Christ as the Messiah, God is no longer bound by the promises He formally made to the descendants of Abraham, Isaac and Jacob. Supersessionism also teaches that those promises of God now belong to The Church-- and only the curses of God continue to belong to the Jews.

I strongly recommend the book *Basic Theology,* by Charles C. Ryrie. It is a wonderful resource for understanding the varying Christian theological views on numerous subjects, including Amillennialism and Replacement Theology.

Answering Fools in Their Folly

Proverbs 26:5

Answer a fool according to his folly, lest he be wise in his own eyes.

There are times we Christian Zionists must weigh in on matters of anti-Israel rhetoric and activities within the Christian community. There are times we must "answer fools according to their folly." The letter to President Bush that I have just referenced presented such an occasion.

In response to that letter, David Brog immediately sent out the following e-mail to CUFI's thousands of supporters, including many national Christian leaders who then forwarded it to hundreds of thousands within their flocks.

MESSAGE FROM DAVID BROG,
CUFI EXECUTIVE DIRECTOR

"Last Friday, a group of over thirty evangelical Christians wrote a letter to President Bush to "correct a serious misperception among some people... that all American evangelicals are opposed to a two-state solution and the creation of a new Palestinian state." They made reference to the "cycle of violence" in the region and the fact that "Israelis and Palestinians must both accept each other's right to exist."

It's no coincidence that this letter was sent barely a week after our second annual Washington, D.C. summit. As we grow, those who disagree with us, however few they may be, will be shouting at the top of their lungs in an effort to equal the sound of 4,500 Christians gathered in the D.C. Convention Center cheering our cause. They will not succeed.

This letter raises many questions. But the biggest question is this-- where have these people been for the past decade? Don't they realize that Israel not only accepted the Palestinian right to exist, but repeatedly sought to give the Palestinians land on which to build their state? At meetings in Camp David in 2000, Prime Minister Ehud Barak offered the Palestinians 100% of Gaza, over 90% of the West Bank, and sufficient land from Israel's Negev Desert to compensate for every inch of the West Bank that would not be returned. He also offered them control of the Muslim areas of Jerusalem. What was the Palestinian response to this unprecedented offer? Celebration? A counter-offer? No-- sadly, the Palestinians chose this juncture to start the second intifada with a spree of bus bombings and killings. In 2005, Israel actually did pull out of the Gaza Strip and left it to Palestinian rule. What did the Palestinians do? Did they take over the Israeli greenhouses left behind and begin to build their economy? Did they take this opportunity to demonstrate that they wanted to live side-by-side with Israel? No-- sadly, Hamas terrorists took over the Gaza Strip and now use it as a base from which to launch rocket attacks against Israel.

The letter's use of the term "cycle of violence" is particularly troubling. There is a fundamental difference between terrorists on the one hand and Israeli and American soldiers on the other. The goal of terrorists is to kill as many civilians as possible, and when they succeed in doing so they celebrate. Israeli and American soldiers seek to stop the terrorists from killing innocent civilians. When our soldiers kill civilians, however few, it is a tragic error. As both of our nations continue to fight terrorists around the world, we must never permit the morally callous equation of these opposite roles.

We all want peace. No one wants peace more than the Israelis who live on the front lines. But wishes don't always come true. To survive in this world, love is important. So is understanding. And so is realism. Sadly, given this track record, only a dreamer or a foe would press Israel for further concession at this juncture. I pray that those who signed this letter are the former.

Pastor John Hagee immediately drafted and is circulating a letter to President Bush, which will demonstrate the widespread support for CUFI's position that America not pressure Israel for further concessions at this time. Beyond this, our best response is

> to continue our work. Let us continue to build and to grow. Let us demonstrate with results that we have the momentum and that we represent the future."

Thank you, David Brog!

There is a time to answer fools in their folly.

There is Hope among Non-Evangelicals!

In CUFI's mandate to gather support for Israel from the Christian communities across our nation, we continue to see wonderful stories of hope spring up from some of the most unexpected sources.

Christians United for Israel is working to set up programs on college campuses all across the nation. Our first CUFI on-campus initiative was birthed at the impressive University of Texas, Austin. The student-staffed CUFI Executive Board of Directors was made up of practicing Jews and Christians, and 95 percent of them were Democrats. An additional and wonderful surprise to us is that almost all our Christian leaders involved on this particular campus were from non-evangelical churches! We are now finding small yet rich pockets of support from non-evangelical pastors and churches around the nation as well!

These are young men and women who have realized the Biblical mandate to love and support the Jewish people outside their own denominational affiliations and theologies.

Answering the question:
"Why don't you educate the anti-Israel churches?"

Here is our painful and true answer: the antidote for the anti-Israel churches within our Christian community is not simply education. We wish it were that straightforward. The anti-Israel attitudes within Christianity are often due to liberal worldviews that have been used to create theological persuasions, which then produce and feed anti-Israel and anti-Semitic prejudices. We will not abandon the necessity to confront the Christian detractors of Israel, nor have we given up on winning them over from their poorly-lit inclinations. Please realize that the difficulty in doing so has more to do with matters of the heart than with education.

We believe our first and most important commission involves the fifty million evangelicals in the United States whom we will continue to gather, educate, and then train so they can become political advocates for the nation of Israel and the Jewish people.

Join us by becoming a member of Christians United for Israel at: www.CUFI.org

I am in Israel seated with CUFI Western States Coordinator Randy Neal, along with Israeli Prime Minister Benjamin Netanyahu and one if his staff members.

Question 6

"How are Christian Zionists trying to influence Israeli politics?"

Standard Christian Answer:

This question will usually get you a very long religious discourse on why the nation of Israel must not give up a single inch of land in the attempts to negotiate peace with its Arab neighbors.

Christians United For Israel

"Christians United for Israel (CUFI) has grown into one of the largest and most politically influential Christian grassroots organizations in the country." –"Bill Moyers Journal," PBS, March 7, 2008

CUFI is a single-issue pro-Israel coalition made up of many diverse and autonomous Christian ministries. One of CUFI's main goals is to turn praying pro-Israel evangelicals into politically active pro-Israel evangelicals.

CUFI's public policy efforts include:

- CUFI's annual Washington-Israel Summit in Washington, D.C., which enables CUFI members to speak personally with their elected officials about their concerns for Israel's security and to express their support of Israel's right to the land by Biblical Mandate.
- **CUFI's** Rapid Response Alerts, which mobilize CUFI members at critical junctures throughout the year to

generate millions of phone calls and e-mails requesting support for Israel from the Administration and Congress.

- **CUFI's** State government efforts. Even state governments can play a role in protecting America and Israel, especially by divesting their public funds from companies that do business with Iran. CUFI will mobilize our members to speak with their state leaders about the need to engage in terror-free investing.

Christian Political Responsibility

Having pastored a church for over 20 years, I understand the Christian leader who states, "The church is not called to be involved in politics."

I also strongly remind those leaders that we are called to be "our brother's keeper," and that the sanctity of life, the historic definition of marriage, and the God-given right of the Jewish people to live in their ancient and promised homeland of Israel are not political issues: *they are Biblical issues!*

Influencing the political policies of the United States government is the responsibility of a U.S. citizen. For Christians, there is also Biblical precedence for participation:

• Moses prayed and petitioned the Pharaoh-- to free the Children of Israel.

• Esther prayed and petitioned the king-- and saved the Jewish people.

• Nehemiah prayed and petitioned the king-- for the rebuilding of Jerusalem.

• John the Baptist prayed and petitioned the king-- concerning the King's unrighteous recent marriage to his brother's wife and his role as a leader. The institution of marriage was not a political issue for John-- *it was a Biblical issue.*

In like manner, the members of CUFI are exhorted to pray and to petition our local and national leaders in matters of concern to the nation of Israel.

It is disingenuous and disobedient for a Christian to say he believes in "blessing the Jews" and yet do nothing to support those words.

James 2:17
Faith by itself, if it is not accompanied by action, is dead.

Sadly, there are many Christians who view any type of political involvement or activism as a waste of spiritual time. The seeds of this apathy and lack of love for our nation have come to fruition as we now witness the disintegration of our national morals that is leading to the frightening collapse of principled reasoning within our society.

Hidden Christian Political Strategies?

Members of the Jewish community often contemplate the possibility of hidden long-term political strategies Christian Zionists may have, including the infiltration of Israeli politics.

My initial introduction to CUFI founder Pastor John Hagee and the immediate aftermath will clarify this legitimate concern. Though I knew very little about Pastor Hagee, what I did know impressed me deeply. I had some knowledge of him from watching his television ministry and from reading about an organization he was starting called Christians United for Israel. I was especially intrigued as I read about his vision for CUFI to become "the Christian AIPAC."

For my Christian readers:

For more than half a century, the American Israel Public Affairs Committee (AIPAC) has worked to help make Israel more secure by ensuring that American support remains strong. From a small pro-Israel public affairs boutique in the 1950s, AIPAC has grown into a 100,000-member national grassroots movement described by *The New York Times* as "the most important organization affecting America's relationship with Israel."

Bashert

For my Christian readers:

Bashert: Yiddish word that means "destiny."

After participating in a panel discussion at the Washington, D.C. Convention Center, my wife and I were whisked through a maze of cavernous hallways and suddenly came upon Pastor Hagee finishing up a conversation he was having with a circle of people around him. We were quickly introduced and almost immediately I experienced the calm pull of Pastor Hagee's presence. After just a few minutes of conversation, he made the following announcement:

"Pastor Victor," he entreated me with his rich and sincere Texas-grandpa tenderness. "I believe the Lord has sent you to be my California Director for Christians United For Israel," he beamed.

Caught completely off guard, I stammered, "Pastor Hagee, it is such an honor to meet you, but I can't be your California Director."

To tell the truth, at that exact time in my life my wife and I had recently been "tossed under the church bus" by a group of Christian leaders and *friends* we had served with for over 20 years. We were so bewildered at what had just taken place in our lives that we had made up our minds to never again be a part of Christian leadership - and were only ministering in D.C. with this understanding with the Almighty.

Bruised battered, and bewildered, my dear wife had officially and permanently retired from her position as a pastor's wife.

My response to her was, "Amen to that 'cause you ain't married to a pastor anymore!"

Apparently, God had not yet received our resignations.

"Well, that's all right," Pastor John answered gently, leaving me feeling as honored as if I had just accepted his unbelievably flattering proposal. "It's a big state, so how 'bout we just cut it in half and make you the Northern California Director for Christians United for Israel?" he pressed onward, grinning at me like I was already printing my new business cards!

"Pastor Hagee, you are breaking my heart here, but there is just no way I can-- " I was interrupted before I could finish.
"No... no, I understand perfectly, Pastor," Pastor Hagee graciously kept me from feeling worse about myself than I already was feeling. "We are all busy men," he acknowledged.

Right. Since then, I've traveled with Brother Hagee; and his busy and my busy are not even part of the same solar system.

"What do you think about being our Sacramento City Director for Christians United For Israel?" he persisted – inching a bit closer to me and smiling like a big, friendly bear.

Recognizing that I was standing before a force considerably more formidable than myself, I sort of lied and answered, "Well, that is something I might be interested in doing. Let me pray about it with my wife and some of my friends back home in Sacramento, and I'll let you know." I think I lied again.

At this time of my life, I was really unsure about…well, just about everything. But I was pretty sure this was going to be the last time I would ever see Pastor John Hagee.

One week later . . .

Just a few days after returning home from Washington, D.C., I received the following letter:

Dear Pastor Victor,

It was wonderful meeting you and your beautiful wife Marita in Washington, D.C. We so look forward to working with you as our **Christians United for Israel California Director,** *and ask that you contact us as soon as possible to let us know where you are at with our proposal.*

I laughed.

I laughed and then considered the fact that we had not prayed about the request from Pastor Hagee. We really had not even thought about it, but now we recognized that we needed to do both. So as my wife and I began to consider the opportunity before us, one day, to my shock, she announced she was "all in." We included our best friends in the fellowship of our decision-making and they too felt I should accept the position. I gathered all the

160

information I could about the one-month-old ministry of CUFI and came up with *only one question that needed answering to finalize my decision.*

The Matter of National Sovereignty

The notion of CUFI becoming a "Christian AIPAC" exhilarated me. Having attended AIPAC conferences for many years and having seen the unparalleled success they had in educating our nation's leaders regarding the nation of Israel, I believed CUFI was being born with heaven's assistance to begin something wonderful and profound between Christians and Jews.

As strongly as I believe in my Christian responsibility to participate in the policy making of the nation of my citizenship, I had great hesitation in becoming a part of CUFI, not knowing the organization's stance on influencing Israeli national policy. I called the CUFI office and spoke with one of its national leaders, Steve Sorenson.

Sorenson served in the United States Air Force Intelligence Community for over 22 years with the Electronic Security Command. He finished his distinguished career as the command's senior Electronic Signals expert, establishing training and evaluation standards for his Air Force specialty. Steve has worked for the last 25 years with Pastor Hagee and serves as the Administrative Director for the Cornerstone Church leadership ministry with almost four hundred groups and five thousand people under his direction.

Without wasting any time, I inquired, "Steve, what is CUFI's position on the pro-Israel Christian movement's attempting to influence Israeli political policy?"

161

"Well, Pastor Victor, there's this little matter of national sovereignty that Pastor Hagee and all of us here have great respect for," he began. "Those are not our children going to war and risking their lives for that nation, and I do not believe we have any right to tell the democratically elected Israeli government how to run their country," he stated with conviction.

"What CUFI will be doing, however, is petitioning the leaders of our nation to neither entice nor coerce the government of Israel into doing anything they do not feel is in Israel's best interest," Steve finished, passionately presenting the official CUFI philosophy on Christian Zionist meddling with Israeli politics.

"Brother, that is really good to hear," I answered, realizing that I had just become the CUFI California Director.

Christian Theology and the Land of Israel

In the never-ending "land for peace" negotiations between Israel and Arab leaders, the thought of Israel changing its borders is attacked with a religious zeal by most pro-Israel Christians and many Jews.

The emotionalism this topic induces is due to a Biblical theology concerning the God-given inheritance of Eretz Israel by the Jewish people.

For my Christian readers:

Eretz Israel is Hebrew for "Land of Israel." When Christians speak of Israel, they may be referring to Jews, the nation of Israel or the physical land of Israel. When Jews speak of Israel, the land, they refer to it as "Eretz Israel."

The theology of God gifting the land of Israel to the Jewish people is anchored in Genesis and confirmed throughout the Hebrew Scriptures.

Genesis 12:7

And God appeared to Abram and said, "To your offspring I will give this land."

Genesis 13:14-15

And God said unto Abram, after that Lot was separated from him: "Lift up now thine eyes, and look from the place where thou art, northward and southward and eastward and westward; for all the land which thou seest, to thee will I give it, and to thy seed for ever."

Genesis 17:7-8

And I will establish My covenant between Me and thee and thy seed after thee throughout their generations for an everlasting covenant, to be God unto thee and to thy seed after thee. And I will give unto thee, and to thy seed after thee, the land of thy sojourning, all the land of Canaan, for an everlasting possession; and I will be their God.

Jeremiah 15:15

As God liveth, that brought up the children of Israel from the land of the north, and from all the countries whither He had driven them; and I will bring them back into their land that I gave unto their fathers.

Lecturing the Jews

The simplified version of this land issue espoused by many pro-Israel Christians-- and religious Jews-- goes like this:

1. God gave the land of Canaan (Israel) to the Jews.

2. Therefore, they must not give away an inch of it to anyone, for any reason.

This sound-bite theology often encourages Christian supporters of Israel to belittle the Israeli government's willingness to consider giving up land in the righteous hunger for peace. The bombastic pretension that we Christians have more political wisdom or a deeper concern for the welfare of the Israeli people than the Israeli people themselves is deeply distressing.

"The day before yesterday, we are told, the Church of the Disciples of Christ demanded that Israel tear down its security fence, which has saved countless of Jewish women and children from being blown to smithereens. Twisting the words of Ronald Reagan, Minister William McDermet III of Panama, N.Y., shouted into the microphone to the assembled delegates,

"Say to Ariel Sharon, 'Tear down this wall!!'"

Well, the Rev. McDermet is either a fool or a demagogue, but I suspect the latter, since even a fool can distinguish between a defensive wall and a prison wall. It is difficult to imagine the towering heights of spiritual arrogance required for an American minister, living fat, dumb and happy 6,000 miles away from any danger, to demand that the people of Israel expose the lives of their children to endless terrorist assaults." --James Lewis

A Sense of How It Feels

On September 7, 2007, Osama bin Laden released another one of his bizarre YouTube lectures to the world. In the video, he appealed to the citizens of the United States to convert to Islam:

"I invite you to embrace Islam. It will also achieve your desire to stop the war as a consequence, because as soon as the warmongering owners of the major corporations realize that you have lost confidence in your democratic system and have begun to look for an alternative, and this alternative is Islam, they will run after you to please you and achieve what you want...to steer you away from Islam."

Christians (and others) were shocked at his self-righteous and preposterous proposition. Consider your emotions upon hearing bin Laden's assumed superiority in his Islamic invitation. Why would anyone entertain leaving his own faith to join bin Laden's political interpretation of Islam that expresses its tenets with the spilling of so much blood?

What could bin Laden possibly have believed that we would find compelling about his expression of faith?

Now consider your emotions in light of our barbaric Christian history with the Jews and you have possibly experienced, in the minutest of ways, how it feels for Jews to be lectured by Christians.

It is my fervent prayer that we pro-Israel Christians practice comprehending the astonishing longsuffering that the Jewish people have endured with us.

I also hope, that before we tell Israelis what they should do with the land of Israel, we might study the complexities of the limited options the leaders of Israel face while attempting to secure peace for their nation. It is naïve and arrogant for U.S. citizens to tell the democratic nation of Israel how it should govern the nation or use the land God has given them.

Standing with Israel

On a recent trip to the Holy Land, my wife and I found ourselves in a small group of national Christian leaders invited by Pastor John Hagee to meet with Prime Minister Ehud Olmert.

165

Our passports had to be examined by the Israeli government three weeks before we were to visit with the Prime Minister, and the on-site search they put us through when we actually arrived at the Knesset building was extensive, to say the least.

Two of the Prime Minister's brilliant young staffers engaged us as we entered the official conference room. While trying to answer all our non-stop questions, they also informed us of the current events of the day. Constantly glancing at their watches, they announced with deferential smiles, "As soon as the Prime Minister steps into the room, we will immediately stop speaking."

Moments later, Prime Minster Olmert entered, and he and Pastor Hagee warmly greeted each other as old friends do. (I am not prone to going all weak in the knees while in the presence of politicians or people of fame, but my spirit was definitely registering this moment as an important one.) Pastor Hagee and the Prime Minister have a long history, and they spoke freely and respectfully with each other. The Prime Minster looked very weary, but his face turned tranquil as Pastor Hagee recounted with passion the recent accomplishments of Christian Zionist support for the nation of Israel.

Toward the end of our meeting, Pastor Hagee smiled and said, "Mr. Prime Minister, we want you to know that the State Department of our government does not always speak for us. If, in the talks with your neighbors, you should ever decide that it is not in Israel's best interests to give up any more land in the hopes of peace – we will support your decision. We represent mainstream America and it can never get too hot for us when standing with you!"

Prime Minister Olmert leaned back in his plush Prime Minster's chair, grinned from ear to ear, and near laughing answered, "Pastor Hagee, you evangelical Christians are the best friends Israel has!"

In the Book of Genesis, Aaron and Hur lifted the hands of Moses as he wearied during the battle with Amalek. We had just lifted the hands and heart of Prime Minister Olmert.

God's Judgment on Dividing the Land of Israel

There is sound Biblical teaching concerning the fulfillment of God's promise to Abraham and his descendants inheriting the land.

There is also sound Biblical teaching that warns of God's judgment upon those who divide the land of their inheritance.

Joel 3:1-2

In those days and at that time, when I restore the fortunes of Judah and Jerusalem, I will gather the Gentiles [nations] and bring them down to the Valley of Jehoshaphat.

There I will enter into judgment against them concerning my inheritance, my people Israel, for they scattered my people among the nations and divided up my land.

Take note: It is "all nations," the Gentiles, who will be gathered and judged for dividing up the land. The land has been given to the Jews to populate, govern, and do with as they will. There is no prohibition warning the Jews against giving up the land.

The boundaries of Israel expanded and contracted during the reign of King David and he was never chastened by the Almighty for allowing the boundary changes.

It is critical for Christian Zionists to petition the United States government to respect Israel's sovereignty in making decisions regarding the security of their nation, including decisions about the keeping or giving up of land.

But the Land Belongs to the Jews!

As a Christian Zionist, the land was always an extremely simple issue for me. For over twenty-five years now, it has held a theologically secure, safe, and uncomplicated place in my heart.

The land belongs to the Jews. Period.

For many Christians, this is a very simple, safe, and uncomplicated issue:

- **Simple** for us because it costs us nothing to believe it.

- **Safe** for us because we don't live there, and giving or keeping the land does not involve the blood of our family or friends.

- **Uncomplicated** for us because our lives never have been personally touched by our theology about the land.

Holding on to simple thoughts is not necessarily a problem. Demanding others to live by our thoughts – now that's a problem.

The Christian pro-Israel movement has zeal to love the Jewish people, but I have observed how we often run out of the gate without knowledge. And as warned in the Scriptures, in our zeal, I fear we sometimes miss the way.

Proverbs 19:2

It is not good to have zeal without knowledge, nor to be hasty and miss the way.

Gaining Knowledge

I received an invitation to spend the day with Dr. Yossi Olmert, brother of Israeli Prime Minister Ehud Olmert.

Dr. Yossi Olmert is a well-known expert on the modern Middle East, Islamic militants, terrorism, the Palestinian issue, and US-Israel relations. He received his Ph.D. from the prestigious London School of Economics and graduated from the Hebrew University *magna cum laude*. Dr. Olmert taught in many well-known universities both in Israel and abroad, including Tel Aviv University, The Hebrew University, Cornell University, City College New York and York University in Toronto, Canada. Dr. Olmert held several senior positions in the Israeli government including Director of Communications for Prime Minister Shamir and Policy Advisor to Defense Minister Arens.

I flew to Los Angeles and found myself sitting around a table with about fifteen other pastors and Jewish leaders, listening to and gaining knowledge from Dr. Olmert. With pained resolve from firsthand experience, Dr. Olmert spoke of the horrors of terrorism and the necessary steps to prevent the ongoing slaughter of his Jewish brethren. He spoke of the "security barrier" and its astonishing effect of reducing successful terrorist attacks.

He told of the 8,500 brave Israeli Jewish citizens who had been living in Gaza and the 15,000 Israeli Defense Force soldiers required to be stationed there daily for their protection. He reminded us of the over one million Palestinians who lived on the same stretch of land and the painful decision to remove the Israeli communities from the area.

"It just didn't make sense anymore," he whispered. "It had depleted our resources and our morale," he almost wept.

"And the nation of Israel has not been born to rule over other people," he soundly reminded us. "The recent consolidation of Israeli citizens out of Gaza was a matter of land for life," Dr. Olmert clarified.

There was no expectation of real peace from this new equation but rather this simple realization: the security barrier saves Israeli lives and stops terrorist attacks. Since construction of the anti-terrorist fence commenced, there has been over a ninety percent reduction in terrorist attacks where construction has been completed.

"The number of Israeli and Palestinian deaths has dramatically dropped– along with the crime of car thefts," he mentioned as an unexpected statistic.

Our hearts were deeply touched with his passion and pain. While sitting at this table, I began to feel knowledge being added to my zeal concerning Eretz Israel. Because of Dr. Yossi, my simplistic, impersonal "land" theology was becoming personal.

The Land God Has Given Us

God has given each of us a land.

It is a land with specific borders, a gift to each of us, and we will one day give an account for our stewardship over it - as will the citizens of Israel for the land they have been given.

Upon the land God has given me rests a wonderful 101-year-old house where my family and I have lived for over twenty years. We love our home, although it rests in a tough, high-crime, inner-city neighborhood amongst a very diverse population. Our neighborhood is not known as a peaceful region. It is better known for gangs and prostitutes, guns and poverty. We do our best, however, to live in peace with all our neighbors, and as Christians we daily try to find ways to show them the love of Jesus.

Our house is right in the middle of one of the largest Pakistani Sunni Muslim communities in Northern California.

Not our plan. God is funny like this with us.

We bought the house (sight unseen) while traveling in Jerusalem and upon returning home to begin the rehab on our new, 100-year-old fixer in the inner city – surprise!

Our Sunni Muslim neighbor's faith is built upon The Five Pillars of Islam.

- Shahadah: is the Sunni Muslim "profession of belief" which is recited daily. "There is no God except for Allah, and Muhammad is the messenger of Allah."

- Salah: is the Muslim requirement to pray five times a day at fixed times: dawn, noon, mid-afternoon, sunset, and nightfall.

- Zakah: consists of spending a fixed portion of one's wealth for the benefit of the poor or needy.

- Sawm: three types of ritual and ascetic fasting.

- Hajj: a pilgrimage to the al-Masjid al-Haram mosque in Mecca, Saudi Arabia at least once in a lifetime for those who can afford to do so. Muslims believe Abram was commanded by Allah to offer up Ishmael at this location.

If you were to close your eyes and walk down our street, the tantalizing smells of curry and sounds of Arabic music often might cause you to imagine you had been transported into a Middle Eastern village.

My neighbors pray five times a day facing Mecca. I am often moved to pray for them when I hear their cars honking as a reminder to gather at the mosque. I have seen them numerous times with their prayer carpets spread in a public setting, should they be unable to gather together during their commanded times of worship.

They pay cash for all their purchases (per Islamic law), including the many properties they own in our neighborhood. Their children are required to memorize the entire Quran by their early teens. The Quran is written in Arabic; their children only speak Urdu and English. They memorize the Quran's 5,000-plus verses phonetically. Some of their women wear burqas (head-to-foot outer covering garments) and all of them cover their heads with shawls whenever they come outside.

They respect our family deeply, and because they have observed our faith as sincere and authentic, they believe we will convert to the Muslim faith "when Jesus returns to rule over the earth."

Yep, when Jesus returns. It is a part of Muslim end of days messianic theology. (See Question 8)

In their eschatological (end of days) view, however, Jesus is Muslim.

Quran 3:45-48

"'Behold!' The angels said, 'Oh, Mary! God gives you glad tidings of a Word from Him. His name will be Christ Jesus, the son of Mary, held in honor in this world and the Hereafter, and in (the company of) those nearest to God. He shall speak to the people in childhood and in maturity. He shall be (in the company) of the righteous . . . And God will teach him the Book and Wisdom, the Law and the Gospel'"

172

Aal `Imran 3:47

"'She said, "My Lord! How can I have a son when no man has ever touched me?"

He said, "It will be so. God creates whatever He wills. When He decides on something, He just says to it, 'Be!' and it is.'"

Quran 4:171

"Christ Jesus the son of Mary was (no more than) an Apostle of Allah and His Word which He bestowed on Mary and a Spirit proceeding from Him: so believe in Allah and His Apostles.'\

As a Christian, I clearly believe differently from these dear and devout neighbors of mine. I love them and pray for them, often with tears. They speak and exhibit their love for me as well.

But what if . . . ?

• But what if rather than being peace-loving Muslims, these neighbors of mine were militant Muslims and had a history of attacking my family and home?

• But what if the lives of my family members were at constant risk of being killed by these attacks?

• But what if I realized that I could no longer protect my family within the boundaries of my home, but I believed that I could protect them if we moved into the teen center, just behind the high wall of our back yard?

One day I began contemplating this comparison of my home and family with everyday life in Israel and the daily decisions their leaders confront in protecting Israeli citizens.

I posed this make-believe scenario to an unsuspecting Christian brother who was in a park, participating in an "anti-Olmert, pro-

Israel" rally (an example of a self-righteous Christian oxymoron from my point of view.)

"How long would you think about moving your family out of your house and behind a backyard fence if you thought it would save your family's lives in this circumstance?" I inquired of him.

"Well," he scratched his chin, wrinkled his forehead, and squinted his eyes in thought. "I'm not sure," he answered, either lying or forgetting to turn his brain on.

"You've got to be kidding me!" I exclaimed incredulously. "If you truly believed your family would be safe behind a fence, you wouldn't think about it for a moment. You would run with them out of the house God gave you! You'd do it because the life of your family is a higher priority before the Almighty than the sticks and stones and dirt of the home He gave you and you know it," I moralized.

Israel's Attempts to Secure Peace

A quick review of the concessions Israel has made over the last sixty years suggests little hope of peace in the Middle East ever being obtainable through politics alone.

• **1947 The Nation of Israel Is Born**: United Nations Resolution 181 recommended portioning the Palestine Mandate between Arabs and Jews. On May 14, 1948, Jewish leaders accepted this solution even though their portion comprised only thirteen percent of the original and earlier British Mandate 1922 and sixty percent of the land now being given to them was in the Negev desert.

• **1947-1948 Israel's War of Independence**: Arab leaders rejected the offer to create another Arab state in the Mandate; less than twenty-four hours after it had become a nation, Israel was

174

invaded by the armies of Egypt, Syria, Transjordan, and Iraq. Miraculously, Israel's army defeated the attackers – but in the fifteen months of war lost over 6,000 Israeli lives–approximately one percent of the total Israeli population. (In American population terms, it would equal 3,000,000 American deaths.)

• **1949-1956 The Fedayeen Terrorist Raids**: Arab terrorists (fedayeen), trained and equipped by Egypt, repeatedly attacked Israeli civilians from bases in Lebanon, Gaza, and Jordan. 1,300 Israelis were killed or wounded in terrorist attacks.

• **1956 The Sinai/Suez War**: Egypt increased its fedayeen attacks, prevented Israeli shipping through the Suez Canal and blockaded the Israeli port of Eilat, violating international law and threatening Israel's economic survival. With the support of France and Britain, Israel captured the Sinai Peninsula and Gaza. Israel completely withdrew six months later when Egypt assured Israel unimpeded navigation and safety.

• **1959 Al Fatah Terrorist Raids**: Egyptian-born Yassar Arafat formed Fatah in 1959 to conduct guerrilla warfare against Israel. In 1965 Fatah adopted "the entanglement theory," which presumed that its repeated attacks would force Israel to respond aggressively against the Arab states hosting Arafat's fighters, thereby escalating the animosity between Israel and the Arab neighbors.

• **1964 Palestine Liberation Organization (PLO)**: The PLO was formed in Egypt, supported by the Arab League as an umbrella organization for anti-Israel militant groups. In 1968, Arafat's Fatah joined the PLO and eventually dominated it. Over the decades, the PLO carried out thousands of attacks against Israelis and others around the world, including the first airplane hijackings.

• **1967 The Six-Day War**: Israel was forced to defend herself when Syria, Egypt, Jordan, and Iraq intensified their terrorist attacks. Egypt blocked the Israeli national waterways and expelled the UN peacekeeping forces. In preparation for a full-scale invasion, the four Arab countries mobilized more than 250,000 troops, armed with over 3,000 Soviet-supplied tanks and aircraft, against Israel's borders. The Iraqi defense minister ordered his troops to "strike the enemy's civilian settlements, turn them into dust and pave the Arab roads with the skulls of Jews." Israel pre-empted their attack and in a six-day battle as miraculous as any found within the pages of the Old Testament, the Jewish people routed the enemy troops, captured the West Bank from Jordan; Gaza and the Sinai Peninsula from Egypt; and the Golan Heights from Syria. Israel also liberated the Old City of East Jerusalem from Jordon, allowing the Jewish people to once again gather and pray at the Western Wall for the first time in almost 20 years.

• **1967 United Nations Resolution 242 and the Arab Summit Conference in Khartoum**: UN Resolution 242 called for the Arab states to: 1) make peace with Israel 2) recognize the Jewish nation's right to exist 3) enter into negotiations to create new, permanent and "secure borders" for Israel. Israel accepted the resolution and the Arab nations immediately held a summit in Khartoum, Sudan-- and answered the United Nations formula with the infamous "Three No's of Khartoum:"

NO peace with Israel

NO negotiations with Israel, and

NO recognition of the Jewish State of Israel.

• **1967-1970 The War of Attrition**: Egyptian President Gamal Nasser ordered attacks on Israelis in the Sinai. During the three-year conflict, 1,424 Israeli soldiers and more than 100 Israeli civilians were killed.

• **1972 The Munich Massacre**: After 1967, Palestinian terrorists attacked Israelis worldwide. In their most public operation, the group Black September held hostage and murdered eleven members of the Israeli Olympic Team at the1972 Munich Olympics.

• **1973 The Yom Kippur War**: On October 6, 1973 – Yom Kippur, the holiest day in the Jewish calendar (and during the Muslim holy month of Ramadan) – Egypt and Syria opened a coordinated surprise attack against Israel. The equivalent of the total forces of NATO in Europe was mobilized on Israel's borders. On the Golan Heights, approximately 180 Israeli tanks faced an onslaught of 1,400 Syrian tanks. Along the Suez Canal, fewer than 500 Israeli defenders with only three tanks were attacked by 600,000 Egyptian soldiers, backed by 2,000 tanks and 550 aircraft.

Caught unprepared, the Israeli Defense Force (IDF) nonetheless managed to fend off this assault, cutting off Egyptian forces across the Suez Canal and pushing Syrian troops back from the Golan Heights.

While Israel was victorious militarily, the human toll was devastating: 2,688 Israeli soldiers were killed in the nearly three weeks of fighting.

• **Yom Kippur War and President Nixon**: On October 6, 1973, Egypt and Syria, along with Iraqi troops, attacked Israel during Yom Kippur, the most holy day of the Jewish calendar. The Arab nations issued a warning that they would stop all oil shipments to any nation that assisted Israel in defense. Several days into the battle, the tiny nation of Israel was facing not only defeat but the real possibility of being "pushed into the sea" as her enemies had vowed. On October 9, Israeli Prime Minister Golda

Meir made personal appeals to the leaders of the European nations. They adamantly refused to help.

President Richard Nixon was wakened in the middle of the night by the ringing of his personal phone. Meir had absolutely no options left and made a passionate appeal for help. Nixon would later recall how he heard "his mother's voice" in the cry for help from the leader of the Jewish nation. Nixon's mother was a devout woman of prayer and would often read to him from the Scriptures. One day she told him "she had been given a dream" about his life. His mother explained in the dream she saw that "one day he would be in a position to save the Jewish people."

As soon as Prime Minister Meir finished speaking, President Nixon knew what he must do. From October 12th through 14th, 1973, the United States shipped 22,325 tons of tanks, artillery, ammunition, and supplies to Israel and saved the Jewish nation from destruction.

• **1982-1985 The Lebanon Way**: After Jordan expelled the PLO in 1970, the terrorist organization entrenched itself in southern Lebanon. During Lebanon's ensuing civil war (1975-1990), PLO attacks on northern Israel intensified. Israel entered Lebanon in 1982 to root out the terrorist group. The PLO was forced to relocate to Tunis. In 1985, Israel withdrew to a security zone approximately four miles wide along the border, and stayed until it unilaterally withdrew in 2000. 95,000 people had already died in the bitter Lebanese civil war by 1982. During this war, Lebanese Christian Phalangists entered the Palestinian refugee camps of Sabra and Shatilla and massacred an estimated 460 to 700 people, including 200 PLO fighters. Although no Israelis were involved in the massacre, an Israeli court determined that Israel and General Ariel Sharon had indirect responsibility for it because the IDF did not stop the Phalangists' entry into the camps.

• **1987-1992 First Intifada**: The PLO initiated the Intifada ("shaking off") after false rumors of Israeli atrocities circulated through Palestinian territories. Palestinians claimed this was a nonviolent uprising, but it quickly turned violent with 27 Israelis killed and more than 1,400 Israeli civilians and 1,700 Israeli soldiers injured. Almost half (1,000) of the Palestinian casualties were caused by other Palestinians in the "Intifada" (internal fighting) among Palestinian factions.

• **1991 Persian Gulf War**: When the U.S.-led coalition fought to get Saddam Hussein out of Kuwait, Hussein attempted to draw Israel into the war and fired thirty-nine Scud missiles into Israel. To avoid disrupting the U.S.-led coalition, Israel did not retaliate.

• **1994 Suicide Bombings in Israel**: Eight civilians were killed in a suicide bombing on a bus in central Israel, a tactic that would increasingly be used by radical Islamic terrorist factions all over the world.

• **2000 Second "Al-Aqsa" Intifada**: A campaign of suicide bombings and terrorist attacks began on September 29, 2000, and continued for over five years, leaving 1,068 Israelis dead and over 7,000 injured, 69 percent of them civilians. Approximately 3,000 Palestinians were also killed in this conflict.

• **2005 Israel gives Gaza to Palestinians** In yet another "Land for Peace" offer to the Palestinian people, Israel removed over 8,000 Israeli citizens from 21 cities in Gaza, and in effect helped to create the first Palestinian State in the region.

• **2006** Gaza held 'democratic' Palestinian parliamentary elections in January and gave the internationally recognized terrorist group Hamas a majority of seats in the Palestinian Parliament.

• **2006 "Acts of War" against Israel**: Upon the removal of all Jews from Gaza, Hamas and other terrorist groups unleashed a barrage of daily rocket attacks into Israel. Within a six-month period after Israel's withdrawal, over 360 Qassam rockets hit the city of Sderot one mile away from Gaza.

Every Jew had been removed from Gaza for almost a year, but on Sunday, June 25, 2006, Palestinian Hamas terrorists crawled through a tunnel from the Gaza Strip into Israel and attacked an Israeli Defense Force base at the Kerem Shalom crossing. Two soldiers were murdered, four were wounded (one seriously), and one soldier, 19-year-old Gilad Shalit, was abducted alive back to Gaza. Two terrorists were also killed in the attack. Hamas took responsibility for the raid, with its spokesman, Sami Abu Zahari, praising its perpetrators as "heroes of the Palestinian people."

Two weeks later, Hezbollah, supported by Iran and Syria, attacked Israel across the internationally recognized Israeli-Lebanese border, killing eight soldiers, kidnapping two, and simultaneously launching a barrage of rockets against civilian towns in northern Israel. Israel responded with a military operation that lasted 34 days. The conflict concluded with UN Resolution 1701, which went into effect on August 14, 2006. The UN hoped that a contingent of international troops would implement both United Nations Resolution 1701 and an earlier Resolution, 1559, which had also called for Hezbollah's disarmament.

Hezbollah refused to disarm or to free the three abducted Israeli soldiers until July 16, 2008, when the bodies of two of the soldiers were returned to Israel in an Israeli-Hezbollah swap for Lebanese prisoners.

• **2011** On Tuesday, October 18, 2011 Israel agreed to surrender 1,027 prisoners-- including convicted terrorists-- in exchange for Gilad Shalit, who had been held captive by Hamas for over five years.

- **2012 Egypt Elects Islamist President on** June 24, 2012 Muslim Brotherhood's Mohammed Morsi was declared Egypt's first Islamist president after the freest elections in the country's history. The "cold peace" Israel had enjoyed with Egypt for 30 years would immediately crumble in the months to come. To stop the increasing terrorist attacks upon its civilian population, Israel was forced to construct a 165-mile security fence along its southern border with Egypt's Sinai Peninsula.

- **2012 "Pillar of Defense"** From 2005 through 2012, the nation of Israel endured over 9,000 missiles launched from the Hamas-controlled Gaza Strip. On November 18, 2012, Israel launched *Pillar of Defense* with the purpose of destroying Hamas and ending their reign of terror upon the citizens of Israel.

Prime Minister Netanyahu (Nov 20, 2012): *"No government would tolerate a situation where nearly a fifth of its people live under a constant barrage of rockets and missile fire, and Israel will not tolerate this situation."*

US President Barak Obama at joint press conference with the Prime Minister of Thailand (18 Nov 2012): *"Let me start with Gaza. Let's understand what the precipitating event here was that's causing the current crisis, and that was an ever-escalating number of missiles; they were landing not just in Israeli territory, but in areas that are populated. And there's no country on Earth that would tolerate missiles raining down on its citizens from outside its borders. So we are fully supportive of Israel's right to defend itself from missiles landing on people's homes and workplaces and potentially killing civilians. And we will continue to support Israel's right to defend itself.*

The following is a summary of the targeted strikes within Gaza during the eight-day operation.

- Six targeted killing operations were launched against top Hamas figures, including Chief of Staff Ahmed Jabari.

Jabari was involved in the terror bombings committed by Hamas after the assassination of Yehia Ayash, "the Engineer," in 1996, claiming the lives of 59 Israelis. In October 1998, after helping execute a terror attack on a school bus in the settlement of Kfar Darom that killed two Israeli children, he was arrested by the Fatah security forces and jailed in Gaza. There he befriended the late head of Hamas in Gaza, Abed al-Aziz Rantisi, who appointed him liaison between the military wing of the organization and its spiritual founder, Sheikh Ahmed Yassin. He was also linked through marriage to the nucleus of Hamas leadership. His son, Muhammad, married the daughter of Salah Shehadeh, a top Hamas military chief who was assassinated by Israel in 2002. His true rise to power came on June 25, 2006, when Jabari sent a Hamas squad, along with members of the Popular Resistance Committee and Army of Islam, to tunnel into Israel. They killed two Israeli soldiers and took 19-year-old Gilad Shalit hostage in Gaza.

- 1,600 targets were struck by the Israeli Air Force, IAF in the Gaza Strip. 980 of the targets were embedded Iranian-supplied rocket launchers.

- 19 senior command targets, operational command centers, and high-ranking Hamas command headquarters were destroyed. 200 of the targets were tunnels that were being used for smuggling weapons.

- 25 weapons factories were destroyed

Hoping for Peace – Fighting To Survive

This dire 64-year historic record must not be defined as Israel's battle for peace, but must be recognized as Israel's battle to survive. Life is the essential issue with God. And to this day, Israel continues to battle for its life.

Israel, America, and Politics

I had the privilege of sitting in the gallery of the House of Representatives while Israeli Prime Minister Olmert spoke to a joint session of Congress in 2006. This was his first visit to the U.S. as the Prime Minister of Israel, and his address to our nation was the most sought-after ticketed event in Washington. Through the wonderful kindness (and contacts) of a dear Jewish friend, I was granted permission to attend.

I was seated in the upper section of the gallery, a tremendous vantage point from which to observe the entire event taking place. Every seat in the majestic and historic hall was filled. The Prime Minister entered to a standing ovation from the members of the Senate and Congress.

I include his opening comments and portions of the passionate and spiritual message he delivered on May 24, 2006:

Distinguished members of Congress, I come here-- to the home of liberty and democracy-- to tell you that my parents' dream, our dream, has only been partly fulfilled.

We have succeeded in building a Jewish homeland. We have succeeded in creating an oasis of hope and opportunity in a troubled region. But there has not yet been one year...one week...even one day...of peace in our tortured land.

Over the past six years, more than 20,000 attempted terrorist attacks have been initiated against the people of Israel. Most, thankfully, have been foiled by our security forces. But, those which have succeeded have resulted in the deaths of hundreds of innocent civilians...and injury of thousands-- many of them children guilty only of being in what proved to be the wrong place at the wrong time.

My parents Bella and Mordechai Olmert were lucky: they escaped the persecution in Ukraine and Russia, and found sanctuary in Harbin, China. They immigrated to Israel to fulfill their dream of building a Jewish and democratic state, living in peace in the land of our ancestors.

My parents came to the Holy Land following a verse in the Old Testament in the book of Second Samuel: "I will appoint a place for my people Israel and I will plant them in their land and they will dwell in their own place and be disturbed no more."

For thousands of years, we Jews have been nourished and sustained by a yearning for our historic land. I, like many others, was raised with a deep conviction that the day would never come when we would have to relinquish parts of the land of our forefathers.

I believed, and to this day still believe, in our people's eternal and historic right to this entire land.

But I also believe that dreams alone will not quiet the guns that have fired unceasingly for nearly a hundred years.

Dreams alone will not enable us to preserve a secure democratic Jewish state.

Jews all around the world read in this week's Torah portion:

"And you will dwell in your land safely and I will give you peace in the land, and there shall be no cause for fear; neither shall the sword cross through the Promised Land."

Painfully, we, the people of Israel, have learned to change our perspective. We have to compromise in the name of peace, to give up parts of our promised land in which every hill and valley is saturated with Jewish history and in which our heroes are buried. We have to relinquish part of our dream to leave room for the dream of others, so that all of us can enjoy a better future. For this painful but necessary task my government was elected.

And to this I am fully committed."

There were times during the Prime Minister's speech that emotionally felt like a Super Bowl due to the outbursts of applause and numerous standing ovations interrupting his powerful message. Sadly, the inability of everyone in the room to understand the Middle East dilemma was visually evident by an entire seating section declining to stand or applaud while the rest of the crowd unanimously did so.

I was not familiar with the seating arrangement of the chamber and asked the gentleman sitting next to me why this one area of the ground floor seemed so strangely opposed to everything Olmert had said.

"Democrats," he bemoaned, shaking his head in dismay.

"They are already posturing on the platform of a 'war-weary nation' for the presidential election in 2008," my gallery mate finished.

How could this entire segment of our nation's government become so defiant to simple truth? So much of the speech seemed to be just rational, non-partisan common sense to me.

I admit my supreme political naiveté.

The remainder of the Prime Minister's words and the frozen indifference of the Democrat's Club seated directly below kept me mesmerized throughout the rest of the event.

Olmert warned our nation and the world as he spoke, "If we don't take Iran's bellicose rhetoric seriously now, we will be forced to take its nuclear aggression seriously later!"

Thundering applause followed but the substantial slice of seats below sat stoically in slumbering silence.

At one point in his speech, the Prime Minster changed direction and stated, "Both our countries share a desire for energy security and prevention of global warming."

It was at this line in Olmert's amazing speech that a senior Democratic Congresswoman apparently woke up and began clapping wildly. And no one followed her lead.

No one.

I felt so bad for her. I really did.

She immediately stopped clapping, quickly glanced to her left and right, and forcing an awkward smile, slouched down in her chair.

(Note to self: This really is "the big house," and when you bomb here, it hurts-- hurts bad.)

The Prime Minister continued his speech:

We believe in the moral principles shared by our two nations and they guide our political decisions.
We believe that life is sacred and fanaticism is not.
We believe that every democracy has the right and the duty to defend its citizens and its values against all enemies.

We believe that terrorism not only leads to war but that terrorism is war. A war that must be won every day. A war in which all men and women of good will must be allies.

We believe that peace among nations remains not just the noblest ideal but a genuine reality.

And then Prime Minister Olmert added to his list of "we believe" a statement he had spoken earlier. Perhaps prompted by the Spirit, he actually repeated the following sentence a second time, and it is not noted in the official transcript of his speech.

"And I still believe in our people's eternal and historic right to this entire land!" the Prime Minister reiterated.

Now try to understand.

This next event all happened in a nanosecond. At the moment Prime Minister Olmert finished repeating this last statement, I felt like the walls in the chamber of congress would cry out, "AMEN and AMEN" in response!

They didn't.

I sensed, certainly every single person at this historic meeting of both houses of Congress will burst out in applause.

And they didn't.

For some unknown reason, I then glanced down on the ground floor and my eyes were immediately drawn to the prominent Democratic congresswoman again. It was possibly my imagination, but I swear she still looked crushed. She still seemed to be slouching in her chair and thinking that no one liked her and she had really bombed. And she hated that, when she had tried to get people to clap about global warming, no one helped her.

I couldn't take my eyes off of her.

"Well, too bad for her, buddy," a Jiminy Cricket conscience-like voice shattered my bleeding-heart trance. "It's time for you to 'man-up' and do what's right in this house!" the thought echoed in my mind.

I happen to have really big hands, and perhaps they were created for just this moment in the history of the universe because all of a sudden, they just started clapping as loud and as fast as they could clap-- all alone. Maybe it was just going to be the Prime Minister of Israel and me, but at least everyone in the chambers would know that we agreed:

"Dwelling in the land of Israel is the Jewish people's eternal and historic right!"

And then a wonderful thing happened.

The guy next to me joined in clapping, and then another person, and another, and another, and then the room exploded in applause!

And someday the entire world will join us.

Everyone Has an Opinion

As we left the historic hall and stepped outside, there was a large gathering of Jewish U.S. citizens protesting. They had hateful slogans on their angry signs against Olmert and his willingness to "negotiate land for peace."

I then saw another crowd gathering.
Christians.

They had a life-sized mannequin of a Santa-Monica-surfer-looking Jesus. (Man, I think He hates it when we do this kind of stuff.)

These Christians were also challenging the arrogance of Olmert in giving away the Land.

The arrogance.

I'm referring to the protestors, not the Prime Minister.

Things I Know and Don't Know

- I know by God's Biblical promise that it is the Jewish people's eternal and historic right to dwell in the land of Israel.

- I know God has put His Name uniquely upon the Jewish people and has made eternal promises to them that He will fulfill.

- I know the security fence built to stop terrorist attacks upon Jewish citizens has saved hundreds of lives so far. If a fence would save the lives of my wife, son, daughter, family member or friends, I know I would want them all to be living behind it.

- I don't know that dividing Jerusalem will bring any peace to the Jewish people in Israel and I know I am deeply distressed at the thought.

- I know there is no one who cares more about the welfare of Israelis than the citizens and leaders of Israel.

God Will Keep His Promises Concerning Israel

On May 15, 1948, the nation of Israel was reborn, and many Jews (and Christian Zionists) believed one of the promises of God concerning the Jews' return to Eretz Israel was being fulfilled. God has vested Himself by uniquely placing His Name upon the Jewish people. Bringing them back to the land that He gave to their fathers is just the start of His wonderful restoration for them.

Ezekiel 36: 22-28

Therefore say unto the house of Israel: Thus saith the Lord God: "I do not this for your sake, O house of Israel, but for My holy Name, which ye have profaned among the nations, whither ye came.

"And I will sanctify My great Name, which hath been profaned among the nations, which ye have profaned in the midst of them; and the nations shall know that I am HaShem," saith the Lord God, "when I shall be sanctified in you before their eyes."

"For I will take you from among the nations, and gather you out of all the countries, and will bring you into your own land. And I will sprinkle clean water upon you, and ye shall be clean; from all your uncleannesses, and from all your idols, will I cleanse you. A new heart also will I give you, and a new spirit will I put within you; and I will take away the stony heart out of your flesh, and I will give you a heart of flesh. And I will put My spirit within you, and cause you to walk in My statutes, and ye shall keep Mine ordinances, and do them. And ye shall dwell in the land that I gave to your fathers; and ye shall be My people, and I will be your God."

When God has proven Himself holy among the Jewish people by providing them cleansing, new hearts, a new spirit, and by filling them with His Spirit, all the nations (the Gentiles) of the world will know the Lord alone is God!

But right now we are somewhere in the process of the Promise.

The nation of Israel is largely a secular nation. God has not yet given the whole house of Israel the promised spiritual cleansing, or the new spirit or the new heart, or filled them with His Spirit. Neither has He yet given them all of the land He has promised to them. And until He does, many Christian Zionists believe whenever the Jews have attempted to take, or keep the Promised Land apart from God's provision it has always been disastrous for them.

Numbers 14:41-43

Moses said, "Why do you transgress the word of HaShem? It will not succeed. Do not ascend, for HaShem is not in your midst! And do not be smitten before your enemies. For the Amalekite and the Canaanite are there before you, and you will fall by the sword, because you have turned away from HaShem, and HaShem will not be with you."

Deuteronomy 1: 42-44

God said to me: "Tell them, 'Do not ascend and do not do battle, for I am not among you; so that you not be struck down before your enemies.'" So I spoke to you, but you did not listen. You rebelled against the word of God, and you were willful and climbed the mountain. The Amorite who dwell on that mountain went out against you and pursued you as the bees would do; they struck you in Seiruntil Hormah.

Answering the Question

How are Christian Zionists trying to influence Israeli politics?

Answer: "We aren't and we won't. We have great respect for Israel's national sovereignty and the democratic process that allows Israeli citizens to elect their leaders.

"We will petition our state and national leaders to supply, support, and stand with Israel. We will also do everything we can to keep the U.S. government from enticing or intimidating Israel into making any concessions that Israel's leaders do not believe are in the best interests of their nation. We believe the continuation of blessings that have poured upon our nation is contingent upon our nation continuing to stand with the nation of Israel."

For my Christian readers:

The incomprehensible thought of having possibly over fifty million Christian supporters of Israel also carries for the Jewish mind the projection of the potential for unspeakable disaster for them. "What should happen in the years ahead if this enormous force for good becomes disenchanted with us?" Jewish observers ponder-- possibly remembering such Christian "support" as Martin Luther's.

"What might become of the free nation of Israel if Christian Zionists choose to negotiate their tourism and political support for 'favorable' decisions from key Israeli leaders?" some Jews must nervously and silently ask.

In light of our heinous historic Christian testimony with the Jews, we must find a way to identify with the gravity of this question-- based on a Jewish perspective. Upon doing so, we Christians may be able to step down from our arrogant pedestals of assumption that lift us into really believing that we care more about the peace of Israel than their nation's selected leaders.

Question 7

"Do you really believe all the Jews are going to Hell?"

Standard Christian Answer:
"Well, the Word of God says…" and a bunch of verses will follow, along with the "Jesus talk."

Let me guess.

You have picked up this book and-- rather than starting from the beginning-- you have turned to this chapter first.

For many Christians, the litmus test concerning the viability of one's "Christianosity" is not based on faith or love, but based on the ability to judge categorically who gets to go to Heaven and who goes to Hell. Thus, you may have turned to this chapter first, to see if the writer of this book is in fact a *real* Christian.

The Birds and the Bees and Faith

God is God, we are not; and He does not need to defend or explain His actions to us. With that in mind, there are some very hard sayings God has given us in both the Hebrew Scriptures and the New Testament that I sure wish He had explained in more detail.

My father once shared a "hard saying" with me.

On a Saturday afternoon, many, many years ago, my family was at the park having a picnic. (In a moment you will understand my need to make clear this happened not just many but *many, many* years ago.)

My mother observed me laughing and pointing at the bizarre antics of a "two-headed dog" (that's what it looked like to me!) that was gyrating around the grassy area of the playground. Shortly after I was able to stop my hysterical laughing, I found myself (at my mother's request) all alone with my father, who appeared to have something very pressing on his mind.

"Victor," he hesitantly spoke my name.

"Yeah, Dad?" I hoped he would hurry as I was sure there were lots more funny things to see and do at the park.

"Your mother and I feel it is time I talk to you about The Facts of Life," he awkwardly continued.

"OK," I sighed, knowing this was probably going to take away at least five minutes of my play day.

Well, as best I can remember, my dad finished up his entire presentation in about three minutes and concluded his fatherly instruction by asking if I had any questions.

"Nope!" I answered, trying to sound convincing as the fun-clock was still ticking.

"All right then, my boy," my dad grinned, hugging me and swatting my rear end as I bounced off in search of adventure.

While watching his little boy walk away, now as a "young man," my father heard me remark to myself, "Man-- I sure am glad *humans* don't do that."

"Open your Bibles, please," the preacher would now say. (I actually told this story on the very first Sunday I ever formally preached. Didn't get asked to preach again for a long time. A long, long, time.)

My point?

My father's "hard saying" concerning the facts of life (in my little-boy world) was easily sloughed off, as I gleefully interpreted it as having nothing to do with me.

Hard Sayings in the Bible

There are hard sayings in the Torah:

Exodus 21:17

One who curses his father or his mother shall surely be put to death.

We can all feel good about that one because none of us really believe that God wants us to execute any child who sasses Mom or Dad. (Apart from a few parents with rowdy teens who are reading this right now).

The New Testament also has many hard sayings, one of which is:

1 John 5:11-12

And this is the testimony: God has given us eternal life, and this life is in His Son. He who has the Son has life; he who does not have the Son of God does not have life.

Central to Christian faith is the atoning death of Christ as the promised redeemer of mankind. Christians believe man is born into sin and can only be redeemed out of it. The verses in I John are just several of many hard sayings regarding salvation that Christians unequivocally believe.

Sort of.

Our community makes exclusions to the doctrine of salvation through accepting Jesus in a number of cases-- especially when such doctrine would painfully touch our lives. One exclusion to our Gospel message of "trusting in Jesus to be saved" theology has to do with the exception made for children getting into heaven. You almost certainly will not hear a Christian pastor preach a sermon that suggests anything other than a merciful God welcoming the souls of deceased children into the everlasting.

Our Bible, however, gives no absolute teaching regarding the final resting place of babies and children. Some of the verses commonly used in attempts to find a concrete answer are:

Matthew 18:1-4

At that time the disciples came to Jesus and asked, "Who is the greatest in the kingdom of heaven?"

He called a little child and had him stand among them.

And he said: "I tell you the truth, unless you change and become like little children, you will never enter the kingdom of heaven. Therefore, whoever humbles himself like this child is the greatest in the kingdom of heaven."

Matthew 19:14

Jesus said, "Let the little children come to me, and do not hinder them, for the kingdom of heaven belongs to such as these."

We add a few more verses and come up with a syllogistic conclusion that looks like this:

All kingdom members must become like children.
All children are childlike.
Therefore, all children are kingdom members.

This type of exegesis is frowned upon in any other portion of our Christian dogma, and is excluded in defining the very similar expression of God's loving desire found in the verses below.

1 Timothy 2:3-4

This is good, and pleases God our Savior, Who wants all men to be saved and to come unto knowledge of the truth.

You will not find Christian theologians making the following syllogistic argument:

Our Savior is all-powerful God.
God wants all men to be saved.
Therefore, all men shall be saved.

The defining of those things "God wants" in the above example will get you a very long explanation concerning the "three wills" of God: His sovereign decretive will, His preceptive will, and His will of disposition. I offer a very brief theological definition of each.

The three meanings of the will of God:

(a) **Sovereign decretive will** is the will by which God brings to pass whatsoever He decrees. This is hidden to us until it happens.

(b) **Preceptive will** is God's revealed law or commandments, which we have the power but not the right to break.

(c) **Will of disposition** describes God's attitude or disposition. It reveals what is pleasing to Him.

So although God is pleased with the thought of all mankind being saved (disposition) apart from a "trusting in Jesus" experience (perceptive), He specifically decrees (sovereign) only the saving of all *children*?

Yes.

This is exactly what most evangelical Protestant Christians believe to be true.

However, when it comes to adults actually receiving the gift of salvation through Christ, evangelicals have no such conformity in our beliefs.

- Some evangelicals believe you have no choice in your belief in Christ: He chooses those whom He desires to be saved.

- And some evangelicals believe you have free will in making the decision to believe in Christ.

- Some evangelicals believe that once you have been born again, you can, based on how you then behave, become un-born-again and be eternally rejected by Christ.

- Yet some evangelicals believe that once you have been born again, Jesus is pretty much stuck with you.

- Some Christian denominations perform infant baptisms.

- Some Christian denominations find the practice of infant baptism heretical.

- And almost every Christian will support the hope that children under a certain unknown age are deemed innocent by God.

Innocent?

My wife and I have raised four wonderful children and have two of the most adorable grandchildren this world has ever seen, and I can tell you one thing for sure: All children (even ours!) begin exhibiting the qualities of obstinate, self-centered little dictators as soon as they realize that crying could be taken to mean "Pick me up now!"

The sinful tendencies of children become increasingly pronounced as these "innocents" enter their single-digit birthdays and learn to vocally express the apparent inborn mantras of "NO!" and "MINE!"

Any religious doctrine I may have concocted concerning the "innocence of children" was dashed upon the harsh realities of actually raising mine.

The widely held Christian belief of mankind being born into sin seems much more likely to be true.

Squishy Christian Theology

This inconsistency regarding the absolution of children within the Christian doctrine of salvation through faith in Christ is essential to soothe our personal concerns regarding the eternal afterlife of the most precious of God's gifts: children. And the reason we stretch and bend our theology so readily in the case of children is that the application of the doctrine touches our own children.

To calm our need for answers concerning God's personal love for us, we have assumed an inferred doctrine called "the age of accountability." The teaching suggests that one who has not reached a certain level of maturity is not held accountable for his sins. Therefore, if he should die prior to reaching this age of accountability, he will enter heaven based on the love and mercy of God.

In other words, he does not enter heaven based on faith in Jesus.

I have a brilliant friend, Pastor Frank Robinson, who is a theologian in the Wesleyan denomination. He perfectly states,

"Determining the 'age of accountability' is a fairly squishy issue; always has been.

"It is not possible for babies and young children to make a saving faith decision regarding Jesus, we Christians assert.

"Therefore, it is not necessary for babies and young children to make a saving faith decision regarding Jesus to enter into the heavenly hereafter, we project."

Once again, this is an inferred doctrine, as there are no scriptures that state God has made special provision to grant deceased children automatic entrance into heaven.

One might think the incongruence between our compassionate escape clause in our kids' salvation doctrine would wither when held next to the scorching proclamation found in New Testament "hard-saying" verses such as:

Romans 9:10-15
Not only that, but Rebekah's children had one and the same father, our father, Isaac. Yet, before the twins were born or had done anything good or bad-- in order that God's purpose in election might stand: not by works but by Him Who calls-- she was told, "The older will serve the younger."

Just as it is written: "Jacob I loved, but Esau I hated."

What then shall we say? Is God unjust? Not at all! For He says to Moses, "I will have mercy on whom I have mercy, and I will have compassion on whom I have compassion."

Even in the face of our own hard sayings such as these, we vehemently resist the possible Biblical truths conveyed by them. We find it easy to say, "God is God, and He doesn't have to explain Himself to us," except when His conduct might actually affect our lives in unfathomable ways.

Christians are left with no choice other than the porous "age of accountability" concept because the thought of our little ones being cast into hell by a loving God is absolutely irreconcilable with our perceived knowledge of His goodness.

For the record, I completely adhere to this non-canon of my faith.

How can I do otherwise?

But should you ask many Christians about the absolute heavenly destiny of Muslim children who have perished; you will probably not receive the same assurance.

Standard Answer: "Well, we know that the Lord is good" or "The Lord looks upon the heart."

Ask about the eternity prepared for the babies and children of the Amalekites written about in the Hebrew Scriptures:

I Samuel 15:2-3

Thus saith the Lord of hosts: "I remember that which Amalek did to Israel, how he set himself against him in the way, when he came up out of Egypt. Now go and smite Amalek, and utterly destroy all that they have, and spare them not; but slay both man and woman, infant and suckling, ox and sheep, camel and ass."

Standard Answer: "That was the Old Testament."

You ask about that poor aborigine in the furthest parts of the outback who dies without ever having an opportunity to hear the Christian salvation message, the aborigine for whom it is not possible to make a saving faith decision about Jesus, since he has never heard about Jesus!

Standard Answer: "I'm not really sure about him, but let's talk about *your* salvation!"

And should a Jew be daring enough to ask a Christian about the resting place of the countless Jewish souls throughout the history of our faiths who chose the option of a torturous death over a forced conversion...

Standard Answer: "The Bible says Jesus is the way, the truth and..." the preaching begins.

But should anyone ask about God's mercy and provision following the death of a baby within a Christian family?

Standard Answer: "Rest assured, s/he is in the bosom of Abraham and gazing into the eyes of Jesus!"

How can we Christians believe this way?

We must believe this way-- but not because our Bible gives us clarity concerning the issue. We ultimately must believe this way because of the white-hot love we have for our children. We ultimately must believe this way because of the intolerable contradictions we face when trying to reconcile a God of love with a God who would cast our children into eternal exile should they perish without a personal faith in Jesus.

Another exception many Christians hold dear regards adult members of our family who die without "confessing Jesus." In the heart-wrenching wrestling over loved ones who have passed on without publicly acknowledging a faith in Christ, many Christians find solace in the hope of a secret grace of God.

Perhaps He offers pardon one last time to the non-Christian relative through supernatural intervention in the very last nanoseconds of life.

We just don't have any Scriptural teaching that would suggest this is the case, so we base our hope on His love-- for those *we* love. Unfortunately, you will seldom hear of Christians entertaining such a belief for the rest of humanity. The doctrine of our faith simply does not allow it, but the love in our heart for those we cherish demands the hope for them.

The Jews and Redemption

At the Israeli Embassy in Los Angeles, my wife and I were to meet with the visiting Israeli Sephardi Chief Rabbi, Shlomo Amar. He was a striking, biblical-looking figure, every bit a member of the priesthood: dressed in flowing robes, crowned with a priestly purple mitre, his long, white beard engulfing most of his face, leaving only his tanned cheeks and gentle, full lips that smiled in concert with his dark, dove-like eyes every time he finished a sentence.

For my Christian readers:

Sephardim are one of the two major groups of Jewry. The word comes from the Hebrew Sepharad, originally the name of an area to which Jews were deported after the destruction of the First Temple. It was first used in the middle ages of the Jews of Spain; after the expulsion from Spain in 1492 the Sephardim settled in North Africa, Italy, Egypt, Palestine, Syria, the Balkans and the Turkish Empire.

The rabbi spoke in Hebrew whispered tones as his translator followed behind and addressed the small roomful of Jewish and Christian guests in English. At one point, while the rabbi took a quick break for a drink of water, our host, retired Israeli General Shimon Erem, stood up at the front of the room and turned around to face all of the guests.

"Now you know, when Mashiach comes, it is going to be just like this," he stated, instantly grabbing our attention.

"He too, will have a translator for all of you Gentiles!" the General belly-laughed.

I think he might be right.

The rabbi finished speaking and thanked all of us for supporting the nation of Israel. He then graciously suggested he would like to answer as many questions as we had time to discuss.

The first guy to jump up was one of ours. Clutching an enormous black leather Bible (King James Red Letter Edition, I'm sure) he waved it around as he spoke.

"Rabbi?" he began.

My wife and I were already squirming. After being a pastor for so many years, you acquire a sixth sense when there is going to be a high cringe-factor moment.

"Rabbi? How do you Jews get forgiven for your sins, seeing that your temple was totally destroyed in 70 A.D. and you no longer have any animal sacrifices?" he slightly sneered.

For my Christian readers:
The Jewish people continue to mourn the loss of their Temple in Jerusalem. Most Conservative and Orthodox synagogues forbid the use of musical instruments during Shabbat services as a continuation of their ongoing sorrow. When speaking with a Jewish leader in my community, she compared the loss of the temple to the Jewish faith to waking up one day and discovering

the sun was gone. "How can we live? What can we tell our children?" she lamented. "Tisha B'Av" is one of the two major annual fast days in the Jewish faith, during which the entire community remembers and mourns the destruction of the Temple.

This Christian Zionist had no interest whatsoever in Jewish theology concerning sin and redemption. His naive mind offered not a question, but a trap, a "gotcha!" moment.

No temple + no sacrifices = no forgiveness of sin.

But Despite All This . . .

This short (thank the Lord!) and naive confrontation with such an honored rabbi is a classic example of a pro-Israel Christian and lover of the Jewish people who does not have one single, cherished Jewish friend. If he did-- he would have known the answer.

Rabbi Amar certainly had more grace for the loaded question than I (obviously) did, as he smiled and offered a brief and sincere Biblical answer, and "schooled" my Christian brother on God's promise to the Jews NOT to abandon them when they are without a temple. My Torah-loving Jewish friends are very aware of their sinfulness before God, and this is not the first time in history they have endured without having their Temple and sacrificial offerings. Christians should remember that after the destruction of the first Temple and during the Babylonian exile, faithful Jewish people continued in the covenantal relationship with the Almighty, and He with them.

Leviticus 26:44

But despite all this, while they will be in the land of their enemies, I will not have been revolted by them nor will I have rejected them to obliterate them, to annul My covenant with them-- for I am HaShem, their God.

Since the destruction of their second Temple and the inability to offer the necessary sacrifices for sin, Jews believe God has made provision for them according to message to them through the Scriptures.

Hosea 6:6

For I desire mercy, and not sacrifice, and the knowledge of God rather than burnt offerings.

Micah 6:7-8

Will HaShem be pleased with thousands of rams, with ten thousands of rivers of oil? Shall I give my first-born for my transgression, the fruit of my body for the sin of my soul?

It hath been told thee, O man, what is good, and what HaShem doth require of thee: only to do justly, and to love mercy, and to walk humbly with thy God.

Yom Kippur: Day of Atonement

Leviticus 16:29-34

This shall remain for you an eternal decree: In the seventh month, on the tenth of the month, you shall afflict yourselves and you shall not do any work, neither the native nor the proselyte who dwells among you. For on this day He shall provide atonement for you to cleanse you; from all your sins before HaShem shall you be cleansed.

It is a Sabbath of complete rest for you, and you shall afflict yourselves; an eternal decree.

The Kohen or High Priest, who has been anointed or who has been given the authority to serve in place of his father, shall provide atonement; he shall don the linen vestments, the sacred vestments. He shall bring atonement upon the Holy of Holies, and he shall bring atonement upon the Tent of Meeting and the Altar;

and upon the Kohanim and upon all the people of the congregation shall he bring atonement. This shall be to you an eternal decree to bring atonement upon the Children of Israel for all their sins once a year; and (Aaron) did as HaShem commanded Moses.

As noted, it is an *eternal* statute for the Jews, to be performed once a year. It is a day set aside to afflict the soul, to atone for the sins of the past year, but only regarding sins against God.

In Jewish belief, though sins against your fellow man are confessed to the Almighty, they can only be truly forgiven by repentance and restitution toward the one against whom you have sinned.

Kol Nidre: For All the Vows

My wife and I attended Yom Kippur at the beautiful Mosaic Law conservative synagogue in Sacramento, California. One of our dearest Jewish friends greeted us and invited us to sit with him. As the service began, he became our spiritual guide through the next two-and-a-half hours of psalms, prayers, and repentance.

Yom Kippur begins each year with the prayer, Kol Nidre, meaning "for all the vows or pledges." This opening prayer on the most holy Jewish holiday seeks forgiveness for any rash vows that may be made to the Almighty in the year to come. The Kol Nidre was in use as early as the eighth century, and originally was considered a means of annulling oaths forced on Jews by their Christian persecutors.

Upon hearing the history and original purpose of this ancient prayer, my wife and I silently wept.

For my Christian readers:

If you have never attended a Yom Kippur service, I strongly recommend you ask permission to do so from a Jewish friend or rabbi. You will find it to be an incredibly intimate and probing spiritual experience. I wish our Christian community had an equivalent expression in our sacraments. The brevity with which we observe our Christian Communion is often unworthy of the seriousness of our transgressions and of our beliefs concerning the cost of our redemption.

A Rabbi Explains To Me

My friend, Rabbi Matt Friedman, of Sacramento, California, explained to me the thoughts of many Jews concerning Jesus:

One of the greatest differences between Judaism and Christianity is the belief that the death of Jesus served as everlasting reconciliation for those who accepted him as savior. Jesus' death provided his followers the sacrificial offering that cleansed his followers of sin and guaranteed them eternal life after death. These beliefs are not surprising considering the Biblical history of atonement of sins through animal sacrifices and the Christian belief of Jesus as being God incarnate on earth.

If the sacrifice of an animal, which is of lower stature than a human, can bring atonement, then the sacrifice of Jesus, who was God incarnate, could bring about a salvation far beyond that which had been considered before. It is at this point that a crucial difference between Judaism and Christianity becomes apparent both theologically and historically. Judaism does not accept the key theological viewpoints that God would appear incarnate on earth, the messiah would have divine origins or that the offering of a human was either allowable or efficacious for the atonement of sins for other humans.

A Rabbi Asks Me

I flew into New York at the invitation of AIPAC for an event in Connecticut along with author David Brog. David and I were joined by AIPAC's Jeff Mendelsohn, who would moderate our panel discussion called 'Friends of the Faith.' All three of us gasped as our chauffeur pulled up to the exclusive Connecticut gated community where the evening event was being held. We entered the circular driveway framing the front of the enormous, stately mansion. There was a long row of young men in white tuxedos parking cars as the guests arrived.

Over 200 people had gathered in the backyard "Garden of Eden" (as one rabbi exclaimed) where gourmet kosher food and wine stations offered the finest culinary treats. The gracious host family requested that everyone be seated in the staging area. Our panel stepped onto a stage equipped with three large director's chairs and hand-held microphones. After some very kind introductions, we were off and running.

Jeff asked David Brog, "Exactly who are these evangelical Christians, and what do they believe?"

David often brings me to tears as he shares (with his amazing intellect and Ivy League education) the basics of the Christian faith, including our belief in the Word of God and divinity of Jesus Christ. David Brog is a "Jewish Jew for Judaism," as he explains it. Though he understands Christian theology, he does not share in our beliefs contained within it.

I felt a responsibility to revisit Christianity's abominable history of persecuting the Jews, after which I asked forgiveness for the two thousand years of wickedness the Jews have suffered from those who have carried our banner.

I attempted to explain to the audience why evangelical Christians today feel it is an honor, a blessing, a privilege and a commandment for us to love and support the Jewish community and those in the land of Israel.

For many in attendance at these events, it was the very first time they had heard of such things.

At the conclusion of the evening, a handsome young Orthodox rabbi approached me. As we shook hands, he held mine with both of his and thanked me for the words I had spoken. Looking directly into my face, he then asked, "Pastor, as a Christian you believe we did not recognize Mashiach when He came. In considering that, where do you believe the Jews now are as a people?"

"Rabbi, first of all, thank you for allowing me to be here tonight and for believing my words were sincere," I answered.

I clumsily began, "There is a Pharisee mentioned in the New Testament, whose name is Saul." (Saul was a Jewish Pharisee who, upon believing in Jesus as Messiah, became the Apostle Paul of the New Testament.)

"I'm familiar with the writings of Paul," he smiled.

I was so busted! I could feel my face flush with embarrassment from my clever bridge-building attempts, but the rabbi's appreciative grin quickly released me from my ignorance.

"Well, first of all," I tried again, "HaShem has been God for a long time, He is very good at it, and He knows all things before they happen. It was no shock to Him that most of Israel did not recognize Jesus as Mashiach.

"And, as you know, rabbi, it's not like you guys were all that nice to some of the prophets HaShem sent your way," I added, while cautiously smiling.

The rabbi gave a little laugh and shook his head, "No, we sure weren't."

"The mystery of Gentile inclusion into the mercies of God is written in Torah and the writings," I suggested as I quoted one brief example:

Psalm 117:1-2
O praise the Lord all you Gentiles, laud Him all you peoples.
For the mercy of the Lord toward us is great!

"We believe, as written in the book of Romans, that because the nation of Israel did not recognize Jesus as their Messiah, God has 'grafted in' the Gentiles who do believe in Him into the Abrahamic Covenant.

"It is an unnatural grafting," I continued, "as we are wild branches and yet have been made part of a good olive tree.

"This next part of my Christian theology is very embarrassing for me to talk about," I confided to the rabbi.

"Why is that?" he asked.

"Our writings teach that some of the natural branches, the Jews, were temporarily broken off. They were broken off so that Gentiles could be grafted in to the promises that were exclusively given to the Jews. The writing then states we were grafted in so that the nation of Israel might become envious, and return to her God," I summarized.

"In our 2,000-year history, envy is not one of the emotions Christianity has provoked within the hearts of Jews," I sadly confessed.

"But you see this as a paternal act of God toward us?" the rabbi earnestly asked.

"I do," I quickly answered, "because it is. You are His first-born!"

"I am very familiar with the chapters in Romans you are speaking about, and will read them again tonight," my new friend smiled as he shook my hand once again.

Answering the question:
"Do you really believe all the Jews are going to hell?"

Answer: Christian theology teaches that the final redemption for Israel and the Gentiles is revealed through the coming of Messiah, a belief many rabbis teach as well. (Upon Messiah's arrival, we can ask if it is His first or second visit!)

Christians have searched the Hebrew Scriptures and New Testament, and have come to believe that Jesus fulfilled every Messianic prophecy concerning the foretold suffering of Messiah, and, that upon His return He will fulfill those of the promised victorious Messiah as well.

We believe God has allowed what we perceive regarding Messiah to remain hidden from the Jews in order that the Gentiles might be "grafted in" to the mercies of God.

The New Testament also teaches:

Romans 11:11

"...salvation is come unto the Gentiles, to provoke the Jews to jealousy.

Salvation has come to the Gentiles to provoke the Jews to jealous? Christianity has provoked the Jews to many things; horror, dismay, abhorrence, hatred... but *jealousy?*

This "new man," made of many nations, was bound together by a single belief concerning Jesus of Nazareth and created by God to bring peace between Jew and Gentile.

Ephesians 2:15

He brought to fulfillment all the commandments and demands found in Moses' Teachings so that he could take Jewish and non-Jewish people and create one new man in himself, so making peace.

In light of our appalling Christian history with the Jewish people, and knowing we have absolutely failed in this Biblically stated purpose of our existence-- I am left with many questions.

I believe the Almighty uniquely loves the Jewish people, and I believe He has made them many eternal promises-- redemption for all of Israel being one of them.

I don't understand how God is going to bring all of these pieces of my faith together; but I believe He will, and I believe as it is written: "All of Israel will be delivered!"

Romans 11:25-27

For I do not desire, brethren, that you should be ignorant of this mystery, lest you should be wise in your own opinion, that blindness in part has happened to Israel until the fullness of the Gentiles has come in. And so all Israel will be delivered, as it is written.

Isaiah 59:20-21

The Deliverer will come out of Zion, and He will turn away ungodliness from Jacob; for this is My covenant with them, when I take away their sins.

Question 8

"You love your enemies? How can you love the terrorists that are killing our children in Israel?"

Standard Christian Answer:

Jesus taught us to love our enemies and so we "hate the sin but love the sinner!" And the 'Jesus talk' begins.

I was invited to speak at a university during their campus Israel Week. Partway through my presentation, I noticed two female Jewish students in an animated whispered exchange. As I looked their way, our eyes met for just a moment, and both of them immediately raised their hands into the air.

"Pastor Victor?" one of them spoke as I acknowledged them both. "You just said that you live within a Sunni Muslim community and you love your neighbors?" she accurately restated my comments.

"How can you say you love the Jews, and also love the hate-filled terrorists that are killing our children in Israel?" she sternly challenged my apparent insincerity.

"Hang on a minute, sister!" I pleaded as I considered her heartrending question. "You are talking about two completely different situations here. The militant men and women who are killing people in Israel and around the world are nothing like the people I live among in Sacramento," I began.

Love Your Neighbor as You Love Yourself

My family and I have lived within a Sunni Muslim community in our neighborhood for over a decade. Among my Christian friends, very few of them have a Muslim friend. As a result, I often find myself a lone voice defending the observant peace-loving Muslim faith community. Even some of the most outspoken of Christian ex-Muslims seem to have only experienced a hate-filled expression of Islam and often whip the sheep of our Christian flocks into a lather with their shrill stereotyping of all Muslims.

I have such great concern for the Christian community and our proclivity to hate.

Let's be honest.

Though there are stellar examples among individuals and many local churches, Christianity is not known for loving. We are not known for loving gays, bisexuals, or transsexuals. We are not known for loving Jehovah's Witnesses, Mormons, and Muslims. Sadly, at this point in history, Christians are not always known for loving one another. Ask any pastor-- or pastor's wife!

I received a phone call from an outstanding Christian defender of Israel. With tears, she pleaded with me, "Immediately sell your house and move!"

This friend and Christian Zionist could not rest until she contacted me; she was so convinced that my Muslim neighbors were just waiting for the right moment to decapitate my entire family.

She doesn't have one close Muslim friend and she has never met any of my neighbors.

My Wonderful Muslim Neighbors

Tiny voices yelling "Vectorrr, Vectorrrr!" from two- and three-year-old Muslim children next door fill my ears and heart with joy every time I walk past them. They shout it out with such pure glee! Until they reach elementary school age, we are the only non-Muslim people most of these little ones will know, and my name is often the first American name they learn.

Their mothers smile and wave to my wife and me as they chatter to each other in Urdu, whenever we pass by their homes on one of our early-evening neighborhood walks. The older adolescent brothers (and sometimes sisters) are at our front door nearly every day asking, "Can we play in the Teen Center?"

We have lived in the inner city for the last 22 years and have always reached out to the kids in our neighborhood. To better touch their lives, we built a Teen Center hangout in our backyard. It has become a "Starbucks/Bible-study/movie-night/slumber-party/birthday-party/pro-Israel-gathering-study-hall/video-game-arcade/Nachos-Night/Sunni-Muslim clubhouse!

Numerous times I have been asked to bring the Muslim boys to the hospital in emergency situations. Twice I have had to sign my name as a family member (their "Uncle Victor") so they could receive emergency stitches and tetanus shots needed. We still laugh about it.

My wife has taxied and assisted many of the Muslim women in the community with their doctor's visits and children's school registration appointments.

On Christmas, we often give gifts to each of the children, and last year we were able to give beautiful handmade baby blankets to each of the (always many) pregnant mothers.

Aziz lives a few homes down from us, and his doorless garage is our local Madrasa. I have spent hours over the years talking with their community leaders-- Aziz and Mohammad, and Mohammad and Hyder, and Habidur and Mohammad-- about their faith in Allah. Through over a decade of personal relationships with these neighbors, I have intimately watched, listened and learned firsthand about their practice of Sunni Muslim faith.

They speak of Allah as "always kind and merciful."

The Muslim mothers and fathers dote on their children and grandchildren as we do ours. They respect our family deeply, and because they have observed our faith as sincere, they believe we will convert to the Muslim faith "when Jesus returns to rule over the earth."

Not the Jewish Jesus of the New Testament, but the "Prophet" of the Quran:

The Prophet said: "There is no prophet between me and him, that is, Jesus. He will destroy the Antichrist and will live on the earth for forty years and then he will die. The Muslims will pray over him." --Sunan Abu Dawood, Book 37, Number 4310

"After his descention [sic] on earth, Jesus will marry. He will have children, and he will remain on the earth nineteen years after marriage. He will pass away and Muslims will perform his Funeral Prayer and bury him next to the Prophet Muhammad." -Tirmidhi, as quoted by Mufti A.H. Elias. Jesus (Isa) "A.S. in Islam, and his Second Coming." www.islam.tc/prophecies/jesus.html

The thoughts of jihad as expressed through militant Islam are abhorrent to them. They view all acts of terrorism committed by people claiming to be followers of Islam as political and as abominations to the Quran and the true teachings of Islam.

When asked about the violence against infidels commanded by Allah in the Quran, my Muslim neighbors explained their convictions concerning those passages. They believe the commands were of ancient times and only against specific people of those times.

Our Violent Scriptures

Our Jewish/Christian scriptures are historically violent. We are all familiar with that old camp meeting favorite:

Psalm 137: 8,9

O daughter of Babylon, that art to be destroyed; happy shall he be, that repayeth thee as thou hast served us. Happy shall he be, that taketh and dasheth thy little ones against the rock.

We learn about the Jewish prophet Samuel's "tolerance" as he executes God's vengeance toward the Gentile king, Agag:

1 Samuel 15:33

And Samuel said: "As thy sword hath made women childless, so shall thy mother be childless among women. And Samuel hewed Agag in pieces before the Lord in Gilgal."

And there is Moses challenging the Israeli officers concerning the guidelines of their holy war:

Numbers 31:15-18

"Why have you let all the women live?" he demanded. "These are the very ones who followed Balaam's advice and caused the people of Israel to rebel against the Lord at Mount Peor. They are the ones who caused the plague to strike the Lord's people. So kill all the boys and all the women who have had intercourse with a

man. Only the young girls who are virgins may live; you may keep them for yourselves."

"You may keep the virgins for yourselves?"
Oh my.

Did you forget about these? just a few of the many examples of bloodshed and violence in the Name of God found within our scriptures?

Speaking Out Against Religious Violence

I have been angrily challenged by a number of friends, "If your Muslim neighbors don't agree with the militant Islamic movement, then why don't they speak out against it?"

I answer with, "Why didn't one single U.S. newspaper print one single Islamic cartoon out of the twelve published in 2006 by the Danish newspaper *Jyllands-Posten?*"

The *Jyllands-Posten* rioting resulted from the September 30, 2005 printing of twelve editorial cartoons, most of which depicted the Islamic prophet Muhammed. Protests erupted across the Muslim world, some of which became violent, with police firing on the crowds (resulting in more than one hundred deaths). Outraged Muslim crowds set fire to the Danish Embassies in Syria, Lebanon and Iran; stormed European buildings, and desecrated the Danish, Dutch, Norwegian, and German flags in Gaza City. While a number of Muslim leaders called for protesters to remain peaceful, other Muslim leaders around the world, including Mahmoud al-Zahar of Hamas, issued death threats.

Many of our most powerful and protected American institutions of free speech, our daily newspapers, claimed they would not print the satirical cartoons out of "respect" for Islam.

None of our television entertainment/news stations showed any of the illustrations, citing the same hollow reasoning.

A nice gesture. If only these same organizations had a track record of showing respect toward Jewish or Christian sensibilities.

I canceled my subscription to our local paper after the editor wasted a half-page of good ink defending the paper's reasons for not printing the drawings. In his pontification about tolerance toward all religious views, not once did the editor of *The Sacramento Bee* mention fear of reprisal from militant Islamic fundamentalists as the real reason for the newspaper's restraint. Nor did the editors of any national paper I read. How transparently dishonest, cowardly-- and, perhaps, smart-- of them.

Until the most influential voices in America find the honesty and courage to fully confront the hate-filled enemies of Israel and the world, why would I demand or expect the neighbors on my block to lead the way?

Monkeys and Pigs?

When talking with my neighbors about the teachings of the Quran referring to Jews as "monkeys and pigs," they acknowledge that these verses exist. Like many Muslims, they believe that these verses relate to a time in Israel's history when the Jews were rebelling against God and rejecting the words of their prophets. It is during these times, they believe, Allah referred to certain Sabbath-breaking Jews as monkeys and pigs:

Suras 2:66 Quran:

And well ye knew those amongst you who transgressed in the matter of the Sabbath: We said to them: "Be ye apes, despised and rejected."

Suras 5:60 Quran

Say: "Shall I point out to you something much worse than this, (as judged) by the treatment it received from Allah? Those who incurred the curse of Allah and His wrath, those of whom some He transformed into apes and swine, those who worshipped evil; these are (many times) worse in rank, and far more astray from the even path!"

Suras 7:166 Quran

When in their insolence they transgressed (all) prohibitions, we said to them: "Be ye apes, despised and rejected."

Let's not forget the writings of the Jewish prophet Jeremiah, and the name-calling even he employed toward the Children of Israel in a time of their rebellion:

Jeremiah 2:24

...thou art a swift young camel traversing her ways; a wild ass used to the wilderness, that snuffeth up the wind in her desire; her lust, who can hinder it? All they that seek her will not weary themselves; in her month they shall find her.

Camels and wild donkeys in heat?

Yikes! Makes "monkeys and pigs" sound almost cute by comparison.

Diversity within Islam

The cover of the *Smithsonian Magazine*, December 2008, asks: "THE SUFI QUESTION: Can the joyous Muslim movement counter the forces of radical extremism?"

A joyous Muslim movement?

Many people have probably never heard of a Sufi Muslim, yet there are tens of millions of them around the world!

The incredibly wide spectrum of Islamic faith expression is as broad and diverse as are the Jewish and Christian manifestations of belief.

According to Raziana Soobratty, "Muhammad predicted that his followers would be divided into 73 sects, every one of whom would go to hell, except for one sect, the religion professed by himself and his companions. However, the number of Islamic sects-- now over 150-- has far exceeded Muhammad's prediction."

Almost none of my Christian friends have any life experience with Muslims other than observing the militant ones reported on by CNN and FOX News stations.

Having said all of the above, I am well aware of the clear and present danger facing the nation of Israel and the rest of the world from the hate-filled proponents of militant Islam. The Muslim Brotherhood, Hamas, Fatah, Al-Qaeda and Hezbollah are just a few of the Islamic religious sects calling for the destruction of the nation of Israel.

Israel's Hate-Filled Enemies

The Muslim Brotherhood

Egypt's 2012 election of Muslim Brotherhood's Mohammed Morsi, was elected as the first Islamist president through the freest elections in the country's history. It is important to recognize that a democratically elected leader does not make a country a democracy. It is also important to recognize that when any society, religious or secular, places wicked leadership into power, the people will suffer.

Founded in 1928 by the Egyptian activist Hasan al-Banna, the Sunni Muslim Brotherhood is one of the oldest, largest, and most influential Islamist organizations.

Egypt has historically been the center of the Brotherhood's operations, though the group maintains offshoots throughout the Arab-Muslim world, including Afghanistan, Bahrain, Iran, Iraq, Jordan, the Palestinian territories (Hamas), Saudi Arabia, Syria and Sudan. It is also active in the United States and Europe.

Islam expert Robert Spencer has called the Muslim Brotherhood "the parent organization of Hamas and al Qaeda."

The Brotherhood was founded in accordance with al-Banna's proclamation that Islam be "given supremacy over all matters of life." Accordingly, the Brotherhood seeks to establish an Islamic Caliphate (a central ruling office of Islam) spanning the entire Muslim world. It also aspires to make Islamic (Sharia) law the sole basis of jurisprudence and governance. Toward this purpose, encapsulated in the Brotherhood's militant credo is: "God is our objective, the Koran is our Constitution, the Prophet is our leader, struggle is our way, and death for the sake of God is the highest of our aspirations." The Brotherhood since its founding has supported the use of armed struggle, or *jihad*.

The Brotherhood supports the waging of jihad against non-Muslim infidels, and has expressed support for terrorism against Israel, whose legitimacy the Brotherhood does not recognize, and against the West, particularly the United States.

"Allah is our objective. The Prophet is our leader. The Qur'an is our law. Jihad is our way. Dying in the way of Allah is our highest hope. Allahu akbar!" --Muslim Brotherhood Motto

- **The Brotherhood's goal is to turn the world into an Islamist empire.** The Muslim Brotherhood, founded in Egypt in 1928, is a revolutionary fundamentalist movement to restore the caliphate and strict *Sharia* (Islamist) law in Muslim lands and, ultimately, the world. Today, it has chapters in 80 countries.

- **"It is in the nature of Islam to dominate, not to be dominated, to impose its law on all nations and to extend its power to the entire planet."** *--Muslim Brotherhood founder Hassan al-Banna*

- **The Brotherhood wants America to fall. It tells followers to be "patient" because America "is heading towards its demise." The U.S. is an infidel that "does not champion moral and human values and cannot lead humanity."** *--Muslim Brotherhood Supreme Guide Muhammed Badi, September 2010*

- **The Brotherhood claims western democracy is "corrupt," "unrealistic" and "false."** *--Former Muslim Brotherhood Supreme Guide Muhammed Mahdi Akef*

- **The Brotherhood calls for jihad against "the Muslim's real enemies, not only Israel but also the United States. Waging jihad against both of these infidels is a commandment of Allah that cannot be disregarded**." *--Muslim Brotherhood Supreme Guide Muhammed Badi, September 2010*

- **The Brotherhood assassinated Anwar Sadat in 1981 for making peace with the hated "Zionist entity."** They also assassinated Egypt's prime minister in 1948 and attempted to assassinate President Nasser in 1954.

- **Hamas is a "wing of the Muslim Brotherhood,"** according to the Hamas Charter, Chapter 2. The Charter calls for the murder of Jews, the "obliteration" of Israel and its replacement with an Islamist theocracy.

- **The Brotherhood supports Hezbollah's war against the Jews.** Brotherhood leader Mahdi Akef declared he was "prepared to send 10,000 jihad fighters immediately to fight at the side of Hezbollah" during Hezbollah's war against Israel in 2006.

- **The Brotherhood glorified Osama bin Laden.** "Osama is in all certainty, a mujahid (heroic fighter), and I have no doubt in his sincerity in resisting the occupation, close to Allah on high." --*Former Muslim Brotherhood Supreme Guide Muhammed Mahdi Akef, November 2007*

- **The Brotherhood sanctioned martyrdom operations in Palestine. "They do not have bombs, so they turn themselves into bombs. This is a necessity."** --*Muslim Brotherhood Spiritual leader Yusuf al-Qaradawi, December 17, 2010*

- **The Brotherhood advocates violent jihad: The "change that the [Muslim] nation seeks can only be attained through jihad and sacrifice and by raising a jihadi generation that pursues death just as the enemies pursue life," said Muslim Brotherhood Supreme Guide Muhammed Badi in a September 2010 sermon.** Major terrorists came out of the Muslim Brotherhood, including bin Laden's deputy Ayman al-Zawahiri and Khalid Sheikh Mohammed, mastermind of the 9/11 attacks.

- **The Brotherhood advocates a deceptive strategy toward democracies: appear moderate and use existing institutions to gain power. "The civilizational-jihadist process...is a kind of grand jihad in eliminating and destroying the Western civilization from within and sabotaging its miserable house...so that it is eliminated and God's religion is made victorious overall other religions,"** reads a U.S. Muslim Brotherhood 1991 document. It believes they can conquer Europe peacefully: "After having been expelled twice, Islam will be victorious and reconquer

226

Europe.... I am certain that this time, victory will be won not by the sword but by preaching and [Islamic] ideology." *--Muslim Brotherhood Spiritual leader Yusuf al-Qaradawi, "Fatwa," 2003*

- **The Brotherhood uses democracy, but once in power it will replace democracy with fundamentalist Sharia law as the "true democracy."** "The final, absolute message from heaven contains all the values which the secular world claims to have invented.... Islam and its values antedated the West by founding true democracy." *--Former Muslim Brotherhood Supreme Guide Muhammed Mahdi Akef, November 2007*

- **The Brotherhood's view of women's rights is to subjugate and segregate women.** The ideal society would include "a campaign against ostentation in dress and loose behavior as well as segregation of male and female students. Private meetings between men and women, unless within the permitted degrees of relationship, to be counted as a crime for which both will be censured...prohibition of dancing and other such pastimes." *--Muslim Brotherhood founder Hassan al-Banna, "Five Tracts"*

- **The Brotherhood will not treat non-Muslim minorities, such as Coptic Christians, as equals.** "Allah's word will reign supreme and the infidels' word will be inferior." *--Muslim Brotherhood Supreme Guide Muhammed Badi, September. 2010*

- **The Brotherhood has anti-Semitic roots.** It supported the Nazis, organized mass demonstrations against the Jews with slogans promoting ethnic cleansing like "Down with the Jews!" and "Jews get out of Egypt and Palestine!" in 1936; carried out a violent pogrom against Egypt's Jews in November 1945; and made sure that Nazi collaborator and Palestinian Mufti al-Husseini was granted asylum in Egypt in 1946.

The Grand Mufti of Jerusalem, Haj Amin el Husseini, reviewing the Bosnian Muslim Nazi SS Division Handzar in November, 1943 in Neuhammer, Germany with SS Brigadefuehrer und Generalmajor der Waffen SS Karl-Gustav Sauberzweig, right, the commander of the division:

Muslim Brotherhood on US College Campuses

The **Muslim Students Association** (MSA) of the United States and Canada was incorporated in January 1963, when members of the Muslim Brotherhood came together at the University of Illinois Urbana-Champaign with the goal of "spreading Islam with students in North America." With 150 affiliated chapters located in the United States and Canada, the Muslim Students Association is the most visible and influential Islamic student organization in North America.

Hamas

228

Hamas is an arm of the Muslim Brotherhood and one of the largest and most influential Palestinian militant movements. In January 2006, Hamas won the Palestinian Authority's (PA) general legislative elections by defeating Fatah, the party of the PA's president, Mahmoud Abbas. This set the stage for the power struggle that ended with Hamas's violent takeover of Gaza.

The principles of Hamas are stated in its charter. Following are excerpts: the introduction to the charter quotes the founder of the Egyptian Muslim Brotherhood, Hassan al-Banna, as saying: "Israel will continue to exist until Islam will obliterate it, just as it obliterated others before it."

The Charter of Allah: The Platform of the Islamic Resistance Movement

HAMAS

Article 13: "Initiatives, and so-called peaceful solutions and international conferences, are in contradiction to the principles of the Islamic Resistance Movement. Now and then the call goes out for the convening of an international conference to look for ways of solving the [Palestinian] question. There is no solution to the Palestinian question except by Jihad. All initiatives, proposals, and International Conferences are all a waste of time and vain endeavors."

Article 31: "Under the wing of Islam, it is possible for the followers of the three religions-- Islam, Christianity and Judaism-- to coexist in peace and quiet with each other. Peace and quiet would not be possible except under the wing of Islam. Past and present history are the best witness to that. It is the duty of the followers of other religions to stop disputing the sovereignty of Islam in this region, because the day these followers should take over there will be nothing but carnage, displacement and terror. Every one of them is at variance with his fellow religionists, not to speak about followers of other religionists. Past and present history are full of examples to prove this fact."

--Muslim Brotherhood Charter 1928 (Unchanged as of 2012)

Palestine Liberation Organization (PLO)

The rebirth of Israel in 1948 and the ensuing wars between Israel and Arab nations profoundly changed the boundaries of Israel as wars between nations do. Founded in 1964 as an organization to create a Palestinian state, the PLO grew in regional and international prominence after Arab armies proved unable to defeat Israel in the Six-Day War of 1967, when Israel reclaimed the Gaza Strip and West Bank.

In 1993, Israeli officials, led by Prime Minister Yitzhak Rabin, and Palestinian leaders from the PLO, directed by Yasser Arafat, attempted to find a peaceful solution to the ongoing terrorist attacks upon Israel. These series of meetings became known as the Oslo Peace Process. An extraordinary moment during these talks came as the content of letters written by Yasser Arafat accepting Israel's right to exist was made known to the world.

Letter from Arafat to Prime Minister Rabin

September 9, 1993
Yitzhak Rabin Prime Minister of Israel

Mr. Prime Minister:
The signing of the Declaration of Principles marks a new era in the history of the Middle East. In firm conviction thereof, I would like to confirm the following PLO commitments:

The PLO recognizes the right of the State of Israel to exist in peace and security. The PLO accepts United Nations Security Council Resolutions 242 and 338.

The PLO commits itself to the Middle East peace process and to a peaceful resolution of the conflict between the two sides, and declares that all outstanding issues relating to permanent status will be resolved through negotiations.

The PLO considers that the signing of the Declaration of Principles constitutes a historic event, inaugurating a new epoch of peaceful coexistence, free from violence and all other acts which endanger peace and stability. Accordingly, the PLO renounces the use of terrorism and other acts of violence and will assume responsibility over all PLO elements and personnel in order to assure their compliance, prevent violations and discipline violators.

In view of the promise of a new era and the signing of the Declaration of Principles and based on Palestinian acceptance of Security Council Resolutions 242 and 338, the PLO affirms that those articles of the Palestinian Covenant which deny Israel's right to exist, and the provisions of the Covenant which are inconsistent with the commitments of this letter are now inoperative and no longer valid.

Consequently, the PLO undertakes to submit to the Palestinian National Council for formal approval the necessary changes in regard to the Palestinian Covenant.

Sincerely,
Yasser Arafat, Chairman
The Palestine Liberation Organization

Letter from Arafat to Norwegian Foreign Minister

September 9, 1993
His Excellency Johan Jorgen Holst
Foreign Minister of Norway

Dear Minister Holst:

I would like to confirm to you that, upon the signing of the Declaration of Principles, the PLO encourages and calls upon the Palestinian people in the West Bank and Gaza Strip to take part in the steps leading to the normalization of life, rejecting violence and terrorism, contributing to peace and stability, and participating actively in shaping reconstruction, economic development and cooperation.

Sincerely,
Yasser Arafat ,Chairman
The Palestine Liberation Organization

Letter from Prime Minister Rabin to Arafat

September 9, 1993
Yasser Arafat, Chairman
The Palestinian Liberation Organization

Mr. Chairman:
In response to your letter of September 9, 1993, I wish to confirm to you that, in light of the PLO commitments included in your letter, the Government of Israel has decided to recognize the PLO as the representative of the Palestinian people and commence negotiations with the PLO within the Middle East peace process.

Yitzhak Rabin
Prime Minister of Israel

The discovery of these love notes being passed between sworn enemies filled many weary and wary hearts with hopes for peace in the land of Israel. However, nearly two decades later and after numerous promises to do so, the PLO has *never* changed its

Palestinian National Charter, which calls for the destruction of the nation of Israel.

Shortly after Oslo II was passed in the Knesset, Rabin decided on a public campaign to rally his supporters. Following the first such rally in Tel Aviv in November 1995, he was assassinated by a Jewish religious fanatic opposed to the peace process. Israelis were horrified, and after a funeral attended by many international leaders, including Arabs, a round of soul-searching and recriminations began.

One of the unanimous agreements reached in the 1993 Oslo Accords required removal of the many clauses within the Palestinian National Charter calling for violence and the destruction of Israel. Though there has been much debate as to the sincerity of Arafat's convictions concerning Israel's right to exist, to this day the rewriting of the Palestinian National Charter has never been accomplished, and a new one was never proposed.

In early October 2002, the Dubai newspaper *Al Bayan* quoted Arafat's Foreign Minister Farouk Kaddoumi as admitting that the PLO National Covenant has never been changed.

Portions of the Present Palestinian National Charter

Article 1: Palestine is the homeland of the Arab Palestinian people; it is an indivisible part of the Arab homeland, and the Palestinian people are an integral part of the Arab nation....

Article 3: The Palestinian Arab people possess the legal right to their homeland and have the right to determine their destiny after achieving the liberation of their country in accordance with their wishes and entirely of their own accord and will....

Article 6: The Jews who had normally resided in Palestine until the beginning of the Zionist invasion will be considered Palestinians....

Article 9: Armed struggle is the only way to liberate Palestine. Thus it is the overall strategy, not merely a tactical phase. The Palestinian Arab people assert their absolute determination and firm resolution to continue their armed struggle and to work for an armed popular revolution for the liberation of their country and their return to it. They also assert their right to normal life in Palestine and to exercise their right to self-determination and sovereignty over it....

Article 15: The liberation of Palestine, from an Arab viewpoint, is a national duty and it attempts to repel the Zionist and imperialist aggression against the Arab homeland, and aims at the elimination of Zionism in Palestine. Absolute responsibility for this falls upon the Arab nation-- peoples and governments-- with the Arab people of Palestine in the vanguard. Accordingly, the Arab nation must mobilize all its military, human, moral and spiritual capabilities to participate actively with the Palestinian people in the liberation of Palestine. It must, particularly in the phase of the armed Palestinian revolution, offer and furnish the Palestinian people with all possible help, and material and human support, and make available to them the means and opportunities that will enable them to continue to carry out their leading role in the armed revolution, until they liberate their homeland.

Article 16: The liberation of Palestine, from a spiritual point of view, will provide the Holy Land with an atmosphere of safety and tranquility, which in turn will safeguard the country's religious sanctuaries and guarantee freedom of worship and of visit to all, without discrimination of race, color, language or religion.

Accordingly, the people of Palestine look to all spiritual forces in the world for support....

Article 19: The partition of Palestine in 1947 and the establishment of the state of Israel are entirely illegal, regardless of the passage of time, because they were contrary to the will of the Palestinian people and to their natural right in their homeland, and inconsistent with the principles embodied in the Charter of the United Nations, particularly the right to self-determination.

Article 20: The Balfour Declaration, the Mandate for Palestine, and everything that has been based upon them, are deemed null and void. Claims of historical or religious ties of Jews with Palestine are incompatible with the facts of history and the true conception of what constitutes statehood. Judaism, being a religion, is not an independent nationality. Nor do Jews constitute a single nation with an identity of its own; they are citizens of the states to which they belong....

Article 23: The demand of security and peace, as well as the demand of right and justice, require all states to consider Zionism an illegitimate movement, to outlaw its existence, and to ban its operations, in order that friendly relations among peoples may be preserved, and the loyalty of citizens to their respective homelands safeguarded.

Article 24: The Palestinian people believe in the principles of justice, freedom, sovereignty, self-determination, human dignity, and in the right of all peoples to exercise them....

Article 30: Fighters and carriers of arms in the war of liberation are the nucleus of the popular army, which will be the protective force for the gains of the Palestinian Arab people.

Fatah

The word *Fatah* means, "conquest, victory, triumph" in Arabic. Fatah, under the leadership of Mahmoud Abbas, is an outgrowth of the Palestinian Liberation Organization. Abbas is classified as a moderate and is the Palestinian "peace partner" with whom Israel is now attempting to negotiate (with the very strong encouragement of the U.S. government).

Fatah, whose full name is the Palestinian National Liberation Movement, was founded in the early 1960s by the late Yasser Arafat and friends of his in Algeria. Fatah was originally opposed to the founding of the PLO, which it viewed as a political rival. Backed by Syria, Fatah began carrying out terrorist raids against Israeli targets in 1965, launched from Jordan, Lebanon and Egyptian-occupied Gaza. Dozens of raids were carried out each year, exclusively against civilian targets.

Fatah's popularity among Palestinians grew until it took over control of the PLO in 1968.

In October 23, 2011, Palestinian Authority chairman Mahmoud Abbas told reporters: "I've said it before, and I'll say it again: I will never recognize the Jewishness of the state, or a 'Jewish state of Israel.'"

Al–Qaeda

Al-Qaeda is Arabic for "the base." The organization by this name is also known as the International Front for Fighting Jews and Crusaders, the Islamic Army, the Islamic Army for the Liberation of Holy Sites, the Islamic Salvation Foundation, The Base, the Group for the Preservation of the Holy Sites, the Islamic Army for the Liberation of the Holy Places, and the World Islamic Front for Jihad Against Jews and Crusaders.

Established in 1988 by Osama bin Laden, al-Qaeda helped finance, recruit, transport and train thousands of fighters from dozens of countries to be part of the Afghan resistance to defeat the Soviet Union. To continue the Holy War beyond Afghanistan, al-Qaeda's current goal is to establish a pan-Islamic Caliphate throughout the world by working with allied Islamic extremist groups to overthrow regimes it deems "non-Islamic" and to expel Westerners and non-Muslims from Muslim countries.

In February 1998, under the banner of "The World Islamic Front for Jihad against the Jews and Crusaders," al-Qaeda issued a statement that it was the duty of all Muslims to kill U.S. citizens, civilian or military, and their allies everywhere. In June 2001 Al-Qaeda merged with Egyptian Islamic Jihad (Al-Jihad) of Ayman al-Zawahiri.

After al-Qaeda's September 11, 2001, attacks on America, the United States launched a war in Afghanistan to destroy al-Qaeda's bases there and overthrow the Taliban, the country's Muslim fundamentalist rulers who harbored bin Laden and his followers.

Osama Bin Laden was killed on May 1, 2011, by a U.S. Navy SEAL team that assaulted his compound in Abbottabad, Pakistan.

Hezbollah

Also known as the Party of God, Islamic Jihad, and Islamic Jihad for the Liberation of Palestine, Hezbollah is a Lebanese organization of several thousand Shiite militants which opposes the West and Israel, and seeks to create in Lebanon a Muslim fundamentalist state modeled on Iran. Its primary mission is to destroy the state of Israel and, in the process, to murder as many Jews as possible. Describing itself as "an Islamic struggle movement," Hezbollah condemns "the Zionist occupation of

Palestine" and candidly states that it "sees no legitimacy for the existence of Israel."

Hezbollah means "Party of God." The Hezbollah founding statement contains a section entitled "The Necessity for the Destruction of Israel," which reads:

"We see in Israel the vanguard of the United States in our Islamic world. It is the hated enemy that must be fought until the hated ones get what they deserve. Our primary assumption in our fight against Israel states that the Zionist entity is aggressive from its inception, and built on lands wrested from their owners at the expense of the rights of the Muslim people. Therefore our struggle will end only when this entity is obliterated. We recognize no treaty with it, no cease-fire, and no peace agreements, whether separate or consolidated. We vigorously condemn all plans for negotiation with Israel, and regard all negotiators as enemies, for the reason that such negotiation is nothing but the recognition of the legitimacy of the Zionist occupation of Palestine."

Hezbollah and its affiliates have planned or been linked to a lengthy series of terrorist attacks against the United States, Israel and other Western targets. These attacks include:

- A series of kidnappings of Westerners in Lebanon, including several Americans, in the 1980's

- Suicide truck bombings that killed more than two hundred U.S. Marines at their barracks in Beirut, Lebanon, in 1983

- The 1985 hijacking of TWA flight 847, which featured the famous footage of the plane's pilot leaning out of the cockpit with a gun to his head

- Two major attacks in the 1990s on Jewish targets in Argentina

- The 1992 bombing of the Israeli Embassy, which killed 29 people, and the 1994 bombing of a Jewish community center, which killed 95 people.

A Voice of Reason?

"Dear friends and colleagues, as you are all aware, mankind is currently facing important, numerous and diverse challenges and I will refer to some of them.

1. Organized attempts to destroy the institution of family and to weaken the status of women:

Family is the most sacred and valuable human institution that serves as the center of the purest mutual love and affection amongst mothers, fathers and children, and as a safe environment for the nurturing of human generations and a fertile ground for the blossoming of talents and compassion.

This institution has always been respected by all peoples, religions, and cultures. Today, we are witnessing an organized invasion by the enemies of humanity and plunderers to destroy this noble institution that is targeted by promoting lewdness, violence and by breaking the boundaries of chastity and decency.
The precious existence of women, as the manifestation of divine beauty and as the peak of kindness, affection and purity, has been the target of heavy exploitation in recent decades by the holders of power and the owners of media and wealth.
In some societies, this beloved human has been reduced to a mere instrument of publicity and all the boundaries and protective shields of chastity, purity and beauty have been trampled. This is a colossal betrayal of human society, of succeeding generations and an irreparable blow to the pillar of social coherence, the family.

2. Widespread violations of human rights, terrorism, and

239

occupation:

Unfortunately, human rights are being extensively violated by certain powers, especially by those who pretend to be their exclusive advocates. Setting up secret prisons, abducting persons, trials and secret punishments, without any regard to due process, extensive tappings of telephone conversations, intercepting private mail, and frequent summons to police and security centers have become commonplace and prevalent."

This speech was given at the September 2007 United Nations General Assembly-- by the madman of Iran, Mahmoud Ahmadinejad.

A Very Bad Idea

The phone call came as I was forming matzo balls for a dear friend's "Jewish penicillin"-- the delicious chicken broth soup with ping-pong-ball-sized matzo balls. Her chemotherapy had caused some severe complications, and her daughter had phoned me earlier that day with a request for a to-go order.

"This is Victor," I answered, my phone cradled between my ear and shoulder as the gooey matzo mixture was cupped in my palms.

On the other end of the phone was David Brog, who announced more than asked, "Victor, you are aware of President Ahmadinejad's upcoming visit to the United Nations in a couple of days? The Conference of Presidents of Major American Jewish Organizations has asked Pastor Hagee to speak at the protest rally."

"That's awesome!" I cheered into the phone.

David continued, "Pastor's schedule is such that he just can't be there and we would like you to go on his behalf."

"Huh?!" I stuttered.

"Wait! Wait!! This is a very bad idea!" I near-hysterically shouted into the phone.

"You'll be fine," David was obliged to tell me.

"And Victor," he added, "Don't mess this up!" Mr. Brog encouraged me as he hung up the phone.

I went into a trance and had a vision of a very important occasion where an organization like NASA is asked to send a world-renowned astronaut to make an important presentation. The astronaut is unable to attend the event. NASA goes into their laboratory and grabs a monkey who once actually did fly around the earth in a shuttle . . . and sends him in the astronaut's place!

With much reassurance from my wife, friends, and CUFI leaders, three days later I grabbed a banana and caught an eight-hour flight to the East Coast.

My entire time in New York was like a dream. There I was, backstage outside the United Nations building with the other speakers waiting to be introduced to the crowd of over 25,000 protestors-- who were surrounded by New York's finest dressed in full riot gear, including some monster-lookin' machine guns.

I won't ever allow myself to forget what I then witnessed.

A parade of attractive young people passing by. A long line of Israeli teenagers briskly walked through a small but shrill anti-Israel protest, and then passed directly in front of me. There were schoolgirls with curling, jet-black hair, holding hands and chattering in Hebrew alongside handsome, ruddy-faced Jewish young men with forthright dark-brown eyes. Together they purposely marched to join their swarming family of thousands in front of the staging area.

I smiled at them, and considered their determined strength and beauty as I heard the voice of history: "Just sixty-five years ago, millions of these young men and women marched into mass graves their brothers and sisters were forced to dig. Today they are being forced to remember, and forced to find an answer for why President Ahmadinejad has been allowed to come into their world to threaten them, and mock the remembrance of their sorrow. These young Jews are also being forced to wonder if *Never Again* is just a delusion."

As I stepped up to the podium and glanced out at the rolling landscape of over 25,000 pro-Israel champions, I spoke the following words with the weight of this history pressing upon my heart.

In the Torah we read how Amalek came and fought with Israel. And Moses, Aaron and Hur went up to the top of the hill where they could oversee the battle. It happened that when Moses held up his hands, Israel was stronger; and when he let down his hands, Amalek was stronger. But Moses' hands grew heavy, so Aaron and Hur supported his hands, one on this side, and one on that side so that his hands remained steady till sunset, and Israel defeated Amalek!

Moses built an altar and called its name *"HASHEM is My Miracle."*
G-d often uses people to help perform His miracles.
I represent one of the 50 million Christian Zionists of America who want to be part of the miracle G-d is performing on behalf of the Jewish people and the nation of Israel. We have joined with you, in

---

242

the battle against you. We want to lift your hands-- we want to be on this side of you and on that side of you. We believe that you are the beloved of Hashem and we bless you in the Name of the G-d of Abraham, Isaac and Jacob.

I have been a Christian supporter of Israel for over two decades, and as I travel the nation speaking before Jewish audiences, I'm often asked, "What is your agenda, what is your <u>real</u> Christian agenda?"

We Christian Zionists of today come to you with broken and dismayed hearts. For over 1,900 years, hordes of those carrying the banner of Christianity have betrayed the Jewish people. Appallingly betrayed you—over and over and over again. We cannot change the past, but we can begin to make amends <u>today</u> for what was done then.

<u>Today</u> we resolve to stand up and speak out in opposition to the anti-Semitic war being waged against the Jewish people.

This is our agenda: we want to stand with you.

There is no restitution we can bring to make up for our sins of the past. We ask for G-d's and your forgiveness, and we promise you this: never again will the Jewish community or the nation of Israel walk alone. Never again, will you say, "There is no one for us."

We believe, and are teaching our children and grandchildren, that according to the Torah, the Psalms, the prophets and the New Testament, the Jews are the beloved of G-d, the firstborn of His brethren, and the "apple of His eye."

We believe as written in Genesis and recorded throughout history, *"Those who bless you will be blessed and those who curse you will be cursed!"*

As Christians we believe the blessings that have poured so mightily upon our nation are contingent upon our continuing to bless the nation of Israel.

All Christians are sternly warned in the New Testament, not to be arrogant concerning the Jews. You are the chosen of G-d, His first love, and we Gentile goyim are clearly His second choice!

It is our daily prayer that the efforts of Christians United for Israel will continue to usher in a new history of support, encouragement and blessing to the hearts of our Jewish friends. Using the words of the abolitionist Henry Highland Garnet, we Christian supporters of Israel cry out to our nation's leaders: "Where is the blood of your fathers? Has it all run out of your veins? Awake, awake; millions of voices are calling you! Our Founding Fathers speak to you from their graves. Heaven, as with a voice of thunder, calls on you . . . Arise from the dust."

The president of Iran is blatantly supporting the Iraqi Shiite militants and continues making shipments of IED's into Iraq. To you members of the United Nations, we entreat you: Arise from the dust! Confront the Iranian economic and political establishment with the immediate and unwavering force of every sanction available.

The President of the Islamic Republic of Iran has clearly and repeatedly called for the destruction of the nation of Israel, and the Security Council simply "condemns" the remarks? We implore the International Court of Justice to arise from the dust and indict President Ahmadinejad for incitement to genocide!

The only way to win a nuclear war is to ensure that it never starts. Iran's President has not limited his threats to Israel. He has also asked his fellow Iranians to "imagine a world without America." This is clearly a threat to destroy our nation.

244

World leaders, we beseech you: Wipe the dust of deception out of your eyes and stop this fanatical dictator <u>now!</u>

Mahmoud Ahmadinejad! Yi'mach Sh'mo! Yi'mach Sh'mo! Yi'mach Sh'mo!

For my Christian readers:

Yi'mach Sh'mo is Hebrew for "may his name be blotted out forever." Every year when the Book of Esther is read during Purim, all the Jewish children shout this phrase every time there is a mention of the wicked Haman. Pretty much the Hebrew equivalent of "go to hell!"

Why was this man not arrested the moment his feet touched down on US soil? I fear for my children and grandchildren.

The world has lost its compass.

The majority of people who listened to Ahmadinejad's opening prayers and speech at the United Nations, as well as his speech at Columbia University during the September 2007, U.S. visit had no real concept of what they were hearing.

The Faith of Mahmoud Ahmadinejad

In 2006 Ahmadinejad had offered a similar prayer during his opening remarks when he addressed the United Nations:

"In the Name of God, the Compassionate, the Merciful. Praise be to God and peace be upon Prophet Mohammad and His Infallible Household and chosen disciples. O God, hasten the reappearance of the Imam of the times and grant to us victory and prosperity. Include us among his followers and martyrs."

Include us among his followers and martyrs? He's not joking.

The 12th Imam

To understand the horror of Ahmadinejad's supplication, you must understand the meaning within the theology of his religion.

Ahmadinejad, along with many other Shiite Muslims, awaits the coming of the 12th Shiite Imam, Muhammed ibn Hasan. They consider him to be the last direct male descendent of the Prophet Mohammed's son-in-law Aliâ, who disappeared in 874 AD.

Ahmadinejad's particular brand of Shiism holds that this 12th Imam, also called the Mahdi, (meaning "Ruler of Time") is living at the bottom of a well in Jankaran, Iran. Followers of this belief drop written prayers into the well to petition him.

"Waiting for the Rapture in Iran"
Scott Peterson
Christian Science Monitor, December 21, 2005

For those who believe, the devotion is real. Tears stream down the cheeks of 2,000 men ripe for the return of the Mahdi, the 12th Imam they expect will soon emerge to bring justice and peace to a corrupt world. Eyes stare upward and arms open wide to receive God's promised salvation. The storyteller's lyrical song speaks of tragedy on the path to salvation, prompting cries of anguish and joy.

As at a Christian revivalist meeting that promises healing and redemption, many weep as they pray for the Shiite Muslim version of the second coming of the Messiah. All Muslims believe in a coming Mahdi as a messianic figure who will destroy the enemies of Islam. Islamic tradition pictures the Mahdi as joining with the army of Muslim warriors carrying black flags. The Mahdi will then lead this army to Israel and re-conquer it for Islam. The Jews will be slaughtered until very few remain and Jerusalem will become

> *the location of the Mahdi's rule over the Earth where all infidels (non-Muslims) convert to Islam and live according to Sharia.*

These events occur prior to a second physical coming of Hadhrat Isa bin Maryam (Jesus, son of Mary), whom Islam believes was a prophet of God from the lineage of Abraham, who will accompany the Mahdi upon his return.

The Quran has several accounts concerning Jesus that are similar to those in the New Testament.

From the Quran Chapter 19:

Relate in the Book the story of Mary, when she withdrew from her family to a place in the East. She placed a screen to screen herself from them; then we sent her our angel, and he appeared before her as a man in all respects.

She said: "I seek refuge from you to God Most Gracious: come not near if you do fear God."

He said: "Nay, I am only a messenger from your Lord, to announce to you the gift of a Holy son."

She said: "How will I have a son, seeing that no man has touched me, and I am not unchaste."

He said: "So it will be: Your Lord says, 'That is easy for Me: And We wish to appoint him as a Sign unto men and a Mercy from Us.' It is a matter so decreed."... Such was Jesus, the Son of Mary: it is a statement of truth, about which they vainly dispute.

Shiite Islamic scholars believe Jesus is coming back to earth soon, to serve as a deputy to the Mahdi who will destroy the infidels.

Imam 8

From the Islamic book Tazkarat ol-Olia: "the Mahdi will come with Jesus, son of Mary, accompanying him."

The series explains. *"This indicates that these two great men are to complement each other. Mahdi will be the leader while Prophet Jesus will act as his lieutenant in the struggle against oppression and establishment of justice in the world."*

It is said that these events will happen before all Muslim believers die, and prior to the Day of Judgment, during which a resurrection of the dead, involving judgment and punishment, occurs. It is after this that Allah establishes his kingdom on Earth, with Islam as the worldwide religion.

Ahmadinejad's Apocalyptic Politics

Ahmadinejad's Shiism teaches that "chaos and bloodshed" must usher in the coming of the 12th Imam. Unlike the Christian and Orthodox Jewish theologies which teach that Messiah will come preceded by waves of immorality, wars and divinely decreed natural disasters, the chaos that summons the Mahdi is wholly the responsibility of human action. Therefore, the one chosen to bring about the conditions that will free Mahdi to come and free mankind would be an eternally revered figure indeed.

In his recently published memoirs, French Foreign Minister Philippe Douste-Blazy relates the story of a meeting between three European foreign ministers together with Javier Solana of the European Union and Iranian President Mahmoud Ahmadinejad. The meeting, which took place at the United Nations on September 15, 2005, dealt with what Douste-Blazy characterized as "the generous European offer" to Iran regarding its nuclear program. Douste-Blazy, a surgeon and a professor of medicine by profession, characterizes Ahmadinejad as stubborn, and describes the meeting as leading nowhere.

Suddenly, Ahmadinejad changed the course of the conversation. "Do you know why we should wish to have chaos at any price?" he asked. "Because after the chaos, we can see the greatness of Allah."

Ahmadinejad has made it clear by the use of his political power that he is a true believer in this Shiite End of Days theology. When he previously served as Mayor of Tehran, he promoted a building project to widen the roads to accommodate the Mahdi's triumphal entry into the city. One of his first acts of office as President of Iran was to dedicate approximately $20 million to the restoration and improvement of the mosque at Jam Karan, near the well where the Mahdi is claimed to dwell.

Ahmadinejad's Apocalyptic 'Destiny'

The apocalyptic scenario of Ahmadinejad's faith must be understood as being intrinsically linked with Iran's nuclear ambitions. When Ahmadinejad insists that Iran's nuclear development program is a peaceful one, he really means it. The great "chaos and bloodshed" ushering in the return of the 12th Imam and a new dawn of Islamic worldwide dominance is Ahmadinejad's peace plan. Ahmadinejad believes he has been chosen to create the cataclysmic events that will beckon the promised Mahdi to return. He defines his nuclear ambition as peaceful since it would give him the power to "wipe Israel off the map," and bring about a nuclear response against Iran that would surely follow.

In Ahmadinejad's aberrant and hate-filled theology, this is how peace shall come upon the earth: nuclear chaos will bring the return of Mahdi, the Muslimization of the world, and finally, Sharia law. The belief in his personal divine importance was best confirmed after his U.N. speech in September 2008, which was laden with references to the Mahdi. Upon his return to Iran he met with Ayatollah Javadi-Amoli, and the two discussed an alleged paranormal occurrence while Ahmadinejad spoke. He related to the cleric:

On the last day when I was speaking, one of our group told me that when I started to say, "Bismillah (with the blessings of) Muhammad," he saw a green light come from around me, and I was placed inside this aura. I felt it myself. I felt that the atmosphere suddenly changed, and for those twenty-seven or twenty-eight minutes, all the leaders of the world did not blink.

When I say they didn't move an eyelid, I'm not exaggerating. They were looking as if a hand was holding them there, and had just opened their eyes. "Alhamdulillah!"(Praise to Allah)

Another portion of Shiite belief is built around a culture of martyrdom. The Shiia assumes that persecution against true Islamic believers will come because of the infidels' hatred of their righteous conduct. Consider Ahmadinejad's speech given to a gathering of families of martyrs in 2006:

"We are all obliged to keep alive the culture of martyrdom-seeking in the society. Culture of martyrdom-seeking is our most effective weapon and best guarantee for our national security. Ruthless enemies who have a chronic enmity against our country and our nation have not succeeded in achieving their objectives so far thanks to the existence of this culture of martyrdom-seeking among our nation. He who is ready for martyrdom is always victorious. Martyrdom is the peak of mankind's perfection and the

martyrs enjoy the highest status of humanity in this world and the Hereafter. People spend tough years of strenuous work in a bid to achieve the peaks of grandeur and pride, while our dear martyrs achieved those high peaks in shortest possible time."

Non-Negotiables of Faith

The leaders of our nation must wake up to the religious ideology driving the political agenda of Ahmadinejad and other militant Muslim groups around the world. The use of martyrdom and weapons of mass destruction is not only entirely appropriate in the minds of these devoted followers of their faith, they are divinely sanctioned and entirely justified.

To hope that religiously motivated zealots can be forced into becoming moderates by talk or sanction is to not understand them at all. Their *"holy* war" against all infidels is central to their Islamic ideology. It is a non-negotiable pillar of their faith.

My Torah-loving Jewish friends will never switch Shabbat to Wednesday, or Thursday or any other day. It is an eternal portion of the Jewish faith. God commanded to keep the Sabbath starting every Friday at sundown, and if you are an observant Jew, Shabbat is Shabbat and that's that. It is a non-negotiable facet of your faith.

For my Christian readers:

Shabbat is Hebrew for Sabbath. Most Jews spend Friday evening holding a Shabbat family dinner where they pray, sing, and bless wives and children. The day of rest ends on Saturday evening at sundown.

Exodus 20:8

Remember the Sabbath day by keeping it holy.

"Christianity's first-century adaptation of Sunday as our day of rest was partially motivated by early anti-Semitism. The Sabbath was re-interpreted by the church in Rome to be a temporary institution given to the Jews as a sign of their unfaithfulness. Christians were encouraged to show their disassociation from the Jewish Sabbath by fasting on that day, by abstaining from the Lord's Supper, and by not attending religious assemblies".

--Samuele Bacchiocchi, Ph.D., Andrews University

Though some suggest that Jesus was simply unconscious when taken from the cross and placed in the tomb, Christians believe He died and was resurrected from the dead. We are unable to change our doctrine of belief into something more rational.

It is a non-negotiable facet of the Christian faith.

We all must understand that there is no negotiating position acceptable to the supporters of the militant Muslim faith apart from the complete and unconditional submission of the non-Muslim world to the rule of Sharia. Our nation's leaders must comprehend and accept diplomacy's absolute impotence when battling against such religious fanaticism.

As the nation of Israel celebrated its sixtieth anniversary, Iranian President Mahmoud Ahmadinejad branded the Jewish state as "a stinking corpse that was doomed to disappear." Shortly after his statement and during the 2008 U.S. presidential debates, two candidates were asked, "If you are the President of the United States and Iran attacks Israel with nuclear weapons what would be your response?"

The first candidate answered, "The United States would respond with nuclear weapons against Iran."

The second candidate stated, "We would respond with nuclear weapons and we could obliterate Iran."

I felt physically sick upon hearing and considering their answers. There is an obvious and ominous problem with the way these candidates answered the question concerning Iran attacking Israel with nuclear weapons.

If Iran has attacked Israel with nuclear weapons, it is too late.

- There is no more Israel.
- 6.5 million Jews are dead.
- 1.2 million Arabs living in Israel are dead and if the United States obliterates Iran, 70 million Iranians will be dead.

The only rational answer to the question of Iran attacking Israel with nuclear weapons is for our nation's leaders to draw a red line on Iran's continued nuclear development and say, "We assure Israel and the world that Iran will never possess a nuclear weapon."

Though there has yet to be a clear "red line" at the writing of this edition, our current leaders are promising to never allow Iran to obtain nuclear weapons. The problem with this promise is that Iran continues to move closer and closer to possessing nuclear capabilities-- with the repeatedly announced goal of wiping Israel off the map.

Loving Our Enemies

I am very familiar with the New Testament teaching of Jesus exhorting us to "love our enemies" and "bless those who persecute us." As a Christian, I believe I am the recipient of God's loving kindness extended to me while I *was* His enemy.

Romans 5:5

...while we were his enemies, Christ reconciled us to God by dying for us.

From this unmerited and merciful love, we have created the abbreviated sound-bite Christian theology of "love the sinner, but hate the sin."

The slogan makes a great bumper sticker and has a nice sound to it, and the worse the crime, the nobler we appear when we suggest "turning the other cheek" and loving an enemy of heinous enormity. But such response is hardly suitable when a monster has blown our own child to shreds, tortured and decapitated our husband, or raped and murdered our wife. When answering the unimaginable pain of another whose life has been ravished with such darkness, our offering that "we must love the sinner, but hate the sin" would be a callous comfort.

There are New Testament examples of Jesus exhibiting abhorrence toward sin and sinners.

John 2:13-16

When it was almost time for the Jewish Passover, Jesus went up to Jerusalem. In the temple courts he found men selling cattle, sheep and doves, and others sitting at tables exchanging money. So he made a whip out of cords, and drove all from the temple area, both sheep and cattle; he scattered the coins of the moneychangers and overturned their tables. To those who sold doves he said, "Get these out of here! How dare you turn my Father's house into a market!"

Luke 17:1-2

Jesus said to His disciples, "It is inevitable that stumbling blocks come, but woe to him through whom they come! It would be better for him if a millstone was hung around his neck and he was thrown into the sea, than that he would cause one of these little ones to stumble."

The best thing to do with anyone who would damage the lives of little ones is to drown them? Jesus not only hates these types of sin, but He also has a very, very, very strong dislike toward the unrepentant folks who perpetrate them.

Psalm 11:5

The Lord tests the righteous and the wicked-- and the one who loves violence, His soul hates.

Romans 12:9

Love must be without hypocrisy. Hate wickedness; cling to what is good.

Proverbs 6:16-19

There are six things the Lord hates, seven that are detestable to him: haughty eyes, a lying tongue, hands that shed innocent blood, a heart that devises wicked schemes, feet that are quick to rush into evil, a false witness who pours out lies, and a man who stirs up dissension among brothers.

I am not suggesting that harboring hatred is ever a Christian alternative to forgiveness. A bitterness toward anyone who has sinned against you will eventually devour you from the inside out. Refusing to forgive someone is like drinking poison-- and expecting *him* to die.

There are times when the Biblically-commanded act of forgiving means releasing our demands for vengeance upon those who hurt us, and committing the guilty party into the hands of God and His judgments. It is a mental and spiritual act that in some cases must be performed over and over again-- every time the pain we experienced from those who sinned against us rises up in our thoughts.

Volumes of books have been written on this theme. *Forgiveness: The Power and the Puzzles*, by Wendell E. Miller, is one of the best I've ever read.

Answering the Question:

"You love your enemies?
How can you love the terrorists that are killing our children in Israel?"

The truly subjective "We must hate the sin but love the sinner" is just one of the blanket, shallow answers given to difficult and painful questions asked by the Jewish community. We Christians tend to preach a theological high road to others, especially when confronted with scenarios that do not touch our lives in a personal way. I conclude with what I believe to be a biblically accurate and compassionate answer to the specific question of loving the suicidal, militant Islamic terrorists whose goals include the destruction of the nation of Israel.

Answer: Followers of the New Testament are instructed to love our enemies. We are also taught, "Our love must not be hypocritical, and to make it such, we must hate wickedness."

I abhor the wicked ideology and actions of the militant Islamic movement. When the last deed of a person's life is a suicide attack upon innocent men, women, and children, I believe God abhors both the act and the person committing it. So do I.

Question 9

"What would you say if a Jew told you he wanted to convert to Christianity?"

Standard Christian Answer:

"Praise the Lord!"

I had been flown out to New York University to give a lecture to a room full of Jewish college students. The one Christian student in attendance did not approve of my answer to her question and had just stormed out of the hall, slamming the door behind her.

"Don't worry, she's one of mine," I grimaced, attempting to negate the awkwardness of the moment. (She was actually a Christian anti-Semite and I had inadvertently exposed her darkened way of thinking to her dismay, disagreement and apparent great disapproval.)

The Jewish college kids had been tough on me as well. The atmosphere had the intensity of physics final as I began my presentation. My "always-work" laugh lines had produced barely a single upturn of the lips from the mass of serious and intelligent young faces staring at me.

I began to realize this was probably the first time most of the attendees had ever been face to face with a real live evangelical pastor.

"What do you think about religious mixed marriages?" a young man wanted to know, with a slightly sarcastic tone seasoning his question.

"The Torah prohibits Jews marrying outside of the Jewish faith as does the New Testament in regard to Christians marrying non-Christians. My wife and I do a lot of premarital counseling, and in the case of mixed religious couples I just can't perform the wedding ceremony," I honestly answered.

The atmosphere in the room changed from understandingly apprehensive to uncomfortably silent.

"How can I ask God to bless something the Scriptures teach is not a blessing?" I rhetorically asked, attempting to clarify my theological dilemma.

My response lit a grass fire of hissing debate that blew through the lecture hall.

"Listen, I'm not the czar of marriage or anything, and people can go to the County Court House and get married to anyone they want, and of course I'll support their marriage!" I loudly and sincerely protested so as not to appear to be the religious jerk I suddenly felt like.

"I just personally feel I can't officiate at a wedding ceremony with mixed-- "

"What would you do if a Jew told you he wanted to convert to Christianity?" another student shouted out, cutting short my answer and immediately ending the whispering clamor in the lecture hall.

I paused for a moment to enjoy the calm and answered with a smug little smile, "I'd send him away three times, my friend."

For my Christian readers:

Jews don't seek out converts. There is an ancient tradition of turning down a potential convert three times, which possibly comes from the Middle Ages, when both a convert and the converter would be executed. Due to the arduous path of conversion, the tradition continues in order to discourage those who are not truly sincere in their spiritual interest of Judaism.

"Well, what would you do if a Christian told you he was converting to Judaism?" the same young man followed up, now smiling.

"He'd still be in the family-- so I wouldn't have a problem with it," I quipped.

Finally a little laughter echoed through the hall. I then answered with absolute seriousness.

"Listen, what a person chooses to believe concerning God is what he or she believes. That's why it's called faith."

From Rock 'n' Roll to the Rock of My Salvation

I recently came across a letter I wrote almost forty years ago. Having just graduated from high school, I wrote this letter to my parents. I listed the "10 Reasons I Want To Be A Musician" in an attempt to explain my dire need to drop out of junior college and join a band with a guy named Eddie.

Edward Gonzales Corkill had just quit the one-hit-wonder band, "Jim Doval and the Gauchos" who had a national hit single called, "Hey Momma, Keep Your Big Mouth Shut." They were regulars on the iconic 1960's television show, *Shindig!*

Eddy heard me play guitar one night at his girlfriend's house and asked if I wanted to join his new band and be a rock star.

So You Wanna Be A Rock 'n' Roll Star?

My parents should have seen it coming. I received my first guitar when I was four years old, began guitar lessons when I was seven, started my first band in the sixth grade, and worked as a guitar instructor at a music studio at age fifteen. It was so obviously my destiny to be a rock star-- but somehow my parents hadn't yet noticed.

Here are a few of my deep thoughts concerning my life at seventeen years old. I can't remember why I wrote in all caps or why I didn't proofread this significant document before handing it to my parents:

- I WOULD LIKE TO BE A PROFESSIONAL MUSICIAN.
- I WANT TO TRAVEL AND PLAY IN CLUBS.
- I WOULD LEARN MORE ABOUT MUSIC THAT I COULD APPLY TO MY PLAYING THAN I AM PRESENTLY LEARNING AT SCHOOL.
- ALTHOUGH I ENJOY GOING TO SCHOOL, I HAVE NO INSENTIVE TO STUDY BECAUSE THE MATERIAL I MUST STUDY IS SIMPLY MEMORIZED FOR A TEST, AND THEN FORGOTTEN WEEKS LATER BECAUSE IT IS NEVER APPLYED TO ANYTHING IN MY INTERESTS.
- EDDIE HAS A LOT OF CONNECTIONS AND HE KNOWS MANY PEOPLE WHO CAN HELP US SUCCED WITH OUR MUSIC.
- EVEN IF THE GROUP BREAKS UP AND I HAVE TO START ALL OVER AGAIN, AT LEAST I WILL BE DOING SOMETHING THAT I WANT TO DO, AND THAT'S WHAT LIFE IS ALL ABOUT.

I remember writing this and reading it over and over again thinking, "Man, maybe I should be an attorney!" It just seemed so convincing at the time.

I left college and recorded some songs with Eddie. We were sure we had another national hit single on our hands with "Stop That Train," a heavy-metal rocker with a great chorus: "Stop that train, stop that train, stop that train from movin': My baby's inside!"

We were not exactly Simon and Garfunkel.

While paying our dues by headlining with Eddie's new band at Yuba City's lavish Kabuki Lounge and Bowling Alley, I was busted by the ABC cops (Alcohol Beverage Control) for being under twenty-one years old. I took it as a sign from the "gods of rock" and left Eddie to go back and rejoin a band with a bunch of my former high school friends.

We all decided to quit our day jobs and move in together. It was 1972 and I was now part of a rock'n'roll commune, living on an old abandoned 140-acre dairy farm with ten of my best friends, traveling around the country playing at concerts and beer bars. We had a large organic garden, horses, goats, ducks, cats, lots of dogs - lots of everything, except money. Our hair got really long and our band got really good and we were living the "Age of Aquarius" dream.

There were many young people of our generation who were still looking for their dream. There were many looking for truth, or looking to "find themselves." Some were even looking for God. I was not a part of any of these groups. I was a professional hippie and only looking for whoever was having a party that night.

Truth, religion, church, God, Christianity? I assure you, none of these things were even remotely on my list of "Things to Do before I Die."

One of our band managers was a member of the Baha'i faith. Though he would often pontificate about spirituality, his life example was so dubious that even within our purple-haze-y worldview, the "truth" that he was peddling found no buyers amongst us.

Jesus Freaks would often accost us as we traveled across the country.

When an eighty-passenger school bus pulls into your little city and eleven people-- all with hair down to their elbows-- stumble into your local hamburger stand, you got trouble. And if you're a Jesus Freak, you got a mission 'cause you literally got a busload of sinners in town.

Jesus Freaks!

We seemed to be prime targets for the young men and women of our generation who had "found Jesus" and loved telling others about Him (whether those others wanted to hear it or not). Some of the passionate preachers of "The Way" left us with the very clear impression that our lives were definitely happier and possibly saner than theirs. Others would say little, but leave us with unsolicited Bibles or Jesus tracts.

Every now and then we would cross paths with common yet extraordinary New Testament believers who would possess a near-irresistible fragrance of hope in the simple story they would tell of God's eternal and sacrificial love for us.

I rejected it all.

My rock'n'roll dream life had long lost its glimmer, but even though I went to bed and woke every morning agonizingly bored with the meaninglessness of my life, I detested and despised the very thought of ever becoming a religious nut.

Although God was most definitely not on my list, apparently I was on His.

On November 10, 1973, during a tour with our band in Ashland, Oregon, I woke up in a hotel room and, feeling the familiar and dreaded weight of my empty life, I prayed to Jesus for the first time as an adult. Opening the nightstand drawer, I pulled out a Gideon's Bible and began reading from the Book of Isaiah. About a month later I had finished reading almost the entire Bible and had concluded a couple of things.

First of all, I believed that Jesus died for my sins. Second, I realized that if I was going to try and hang out with Him and His Father, I really needed to change some of my ways or I was probably going to be in big trouble. I called a band meeting and announced to my band mates, "I think I'm a Christian now and there are a few things I'm pretty sure I shouldn't be doing any more."

My friends rolled their eyes, moaned and giggled, and told me I was going to be all right. One year later, as we began our last concert tour together, each member of the band had come to a faith in Christ.

Thirty-nine Years Later

Over thirty-nine years later, a number of us still eat dinner together on Friday nights. We usually light a few candles, thank the Lord for our families, sing from the Psalms, pray for our children (and grandchildren!), and pray for one another.

We also pray for the peace of Jerusalem and blessings upon the Jewish people. None of us are Jewish; we are goyim through and through. We jokingly refer to our Friday night Shabbat gatherings as our "goy-bat" celebration. But we, like millions of evangelical Christians across the nation, have been taught from the Scriptures: Though God loves everyone, He loved the Jews first.

We believe the Jews are a unique and very precious people in the heart of God.

Christian Conversion

We have a saying: "Going to McDonalds doesn't make you a hamburger and going to church doesn't make you a Christian."

I share my conversion story in order to clarify what the experience means in evangelical Christian vernacular. The only steps to becoming a Christian within Protestant theology are within the heart of the one seeking out the claims of Jesus Christ. The act of personally trusting in His death and resurrection as the means of acquiring righteousness before God is the Christian definition of being "born again."

Evangelicals identify with the pardon of God through faith in Christ, similar to the crediting of righteousness by faith granted to Abram in the Book of Genesis.

Genesis 15:5-6

And He took him outside, and said "Gaze now toward the Heavens, and count the stars if you are able to count them!" And He said to him, "So shall your offspring be!" And he trusted in HaShem, and He credited it to him as righteousness.

Ephesians 2:8-9

For by grace you have been saved through faith; and that not of yourselves, it is the gift of God; not as a result of works, so that no one may boast.

Coming to believe God personally knows and loves you can be a bit life-changing to a rock'n'roll hippie-- or to anyone for that matter. Telling others about your life-changing discovery is hard not to do.

The Jesus Freaks who often "harshed our mellow" (irked us) in their sharing the "Good News" during our hippie days were simply telling us their life-changing B.C.-to-A.D. story. It didn't always sound like good news to us, but that generally depended on the maturity and motivation of the messengers.

From David Brog's book, *Standing With Israel:*

While most Jews are aware of the centuries of pain caused by Christian efforts to convert them, few evangelicals are as well versed in their Jewish history. For evangelicals, sharing the gospel comes as naturally as sharing a hidden treasure: they have found something that has brought them great joy, and with the best of intentions they want to pass it on. What Jews call proselytizing, evangelicals earnestly call "sharing the good news." Most evangelicals cannot imagine that someone would take offense at such a gesture. Sensitivity here, as in so many instances, must be taught.

And the teachers, the ones sharing the Jewish perspective with the evangelical grassroots, are typically those who have come to understand these concerns through their close collaboration with the Jews.

In the blessing and cauldron of our two faiths being drawn together, genuine relationships are being forged. Within many of these new relations, I believe true Christian love and respect are replacing historic Christian hatred and perversity. Christians and Jews are becoming friends and as in all intimate friendships, the shallow, old, dusty taboos against discussing politics and religion are swept away.

One such friendship I have is with Fred Hayward. Every time we sit down together we talk like a couple of fifteen-year-old girls on Red Bull. And because we talk, we talk a lot about everything that is important to us. We talk about every facet of our lives. The fact that Fred is a Jew makes all things Jewish a central part of his life, and there are times when we discuss the Jewish faith. The fact that I am a Christian makes faith one of the central portions of my life, and there are times when we discuss the Christian faith. Fred has heard the "good news" from me-- not because of a belief on my part that I can convert him, but as an outgrowth of our genuine friendship. I am delighted by how he sums up the receiving end of his friendship with Christians. In an e-mail responding to *The New York Times* concerning a Christian Zionist article they published, Fred wrote:

I am a Jew who has gotten to know (and love) several Christian Zionists in my city. They have never tried to convert me in preparation for "The Rapture." It is simply not part of their theology. Indeed, their unconditional honoring of my heritage has led me to be more 'Jewish.' And, they have never failed to be there for me, always without asking, whenever they thought I might need some help.

Fred Hayward
Sacramento, CA.

The Jew's "Good News"

Although it is possible for a Gentile to convert into the Jewish faith, it is not necessary in Jewish theology for Gentiles to do so to be deemed righteous before God.

The Jews preach a "good news" message to the Gentiles called the Seven Noahide Laws. Most of my Torah-loving Jewish friends bring this up early (and often) in our relationship as they believe it is God's commanded way for non-Jews to "merit a share in the World to Come," the Jewish equivalent of heaven.

They share their convictions with me concerning my eternal future because of their concern and love for me.

> ### *For my Christian readers:*
>
> Anyone who accepts upon himself the fulfillment of these Seven Mitzvos [commandments] and is precise in their observance is considered one of the Hasidei Umot Ha'olam (Righteous of the nations of the world) and will merit a share in the world to come.

The Seven Noahide Laws

1. Do not murder.
2. Do not steal.
3. Do not worship false gods.
4. Do not be sexually immoral.
5. Do not eat a limb from a live animal.
6. Do not curse God.
7. Do set up courts and bring offenders to justice.

I am honored to spend many hours learning with Rabbi Mendy Cohen, Sacramento Chabad Director. I told him I was pleased to report that I found myself to be reasonably observant of the Noahide Laws– and absolutely aghast at the very thought of one of them in particular.

"Rabbi, who in the world would eat a limb from a living animal?" I squeamishly groaned.

"A hungry hunter," he taught me, smiling.

For my Christian readers:

Chabad-Lubavitch (also known as Chabad, Habad or Lubavitch), is one of the largest branches of Hasidic Judaism and one of the largest Jewish movements worldwide, especially in the United States, the Former Soviet Union, Europe and Israel. Chabad is a Hebrew acronym for *Chochmah, Binah, Da'at* ("wisdom, understanding, knowledge.")

Jewish tradition teaches that God gave six of these seven laws to Adam in the Garden of Eden, then presented them to all humanity through Noah, and reiterated them within the Oral Torah at Mt. Sinai to the children of Israel.

For my Christian readers:

The Written Law is another name for the Torah, the first five books of the Bible. The Oral Law is the Jewish legal commentary on the Torah, explaining how its commandments are to be carried out.

It is possible that the early New Testament Jewish believers in Jesus are referencing these Noahide principles while attempting to give guidance to the first Gentile Christians:

Acts 15:19-20

It is my judgment, therefore, that we should not make it difficult for the Gentiles who are turning to God. Instead we should write to them, telling them to abstain from food polluted by idols, from sexual immorality, from the meat of strangled animals and from blood.

It is remarkable to see our nation's recognition of the Noahide Laws, along with one of the most influential and prolific figures in 20th century Judaism, Rabbi Menachem Mendel Schneerson (1902-1994).

Affectionately called "The Rebbe," Schneerson expanded the Chabad-Lubavitch from a small Jewish sect to a large, powerful religious movement.

In March 1991, the U.S. Congress passed a Joint House Resolution (H.J. 104) recognizing the significance of the Noahide Laws and commending the Lubavitch Rebbe for his educational outreach.

Who Is A Jew?

Traditional Judaism holds that a Jew is anyone born to a Jewish mother or converted to Judaism in a *halakhic* manner (according to Jewish law). Although the Torah does not specifically acknowledge matrilineal descent as being the bloodline recognized by the Almighty for determining true Jewishness, there are a number of verses referenced by Jewish sages suggesting that children with Gentile fathers and Jewish mothers are considered Jews. One of them is found in the Book of Leviticus.

Leviticus 24:10-20:

Now the son of an Israelite woman, whose father was an Egyptian, went out among the sons of Israel...

On the other hand, when dealing with Jewish fathers in Ezra 10:2-3, the Jews returning to Israel vowed to "put away" their non-Jewish wives and the children born to those wives. If these children were Jewish as the sages teach, they would not have been put away.

Ezra 10:2-3:

Shecaniah the son of Jehiel, one of the sons of Elam, said to Ezra, "We have been unfaithful to our God and have married foreign women from the peoples of the land; yet now there is hope for Israel in spite of this. So now let us make a covenant with our God to put away all the wives and their children, according to the counsel of my lord and of those who tremble at the commandment of our God; and let it be done according to the law.

The other point of view in this discussion is articulated well by Shaye Cohen, Professor of Hebrew Literature and Philosophy in the Department of Near Eastern Languages and Civilizations of Harvard University:

Numerous Israelite heroes and kings married foreign women: for example, Judah married a Canaanite, Joseph an Egyptian; Moses a Midianite and an Ethiopian, David a Philistine, and Solomon, women of every description. By her marriage with an Israelite man, a foreign woman joined the clan, people, and religion of her husband. It never occurred to anyone in pre-exilic times to argue that such marriages were null and void, that foreign women must "convert" to Judaism, or that the offspring of the marriage were not Israelite if the women did not convert.

Nevertheless, some time during the Roman occupation and the Second Temple period, a law of matrilineal descent was adopted, and by the 2nd century AD, it was universally accepted.

Answering the question:

"What would you say if a Jew told you he wanted to convert to Christianity?"

My answer: I would first inquire *why* my Jewish friend had interest in the Christian faith. It is a costly and painful one for a Jew to follow, and not something you impulsively "decide to do." I came to faith through the reading of the Bible and would encourage my Jewish friend to do the same, including the New Testament. And though I would explain my understanding of the Christian faith, I believe it is God alone who can give revelation concerning the things I believe to be true concerning Jesus of Nazareth.

V. Styrsky circa 1973

Question 10

"What is your deepest prayer for the Jewish people?"
Standard Christian Answer:
Definitely the 'Jesus talk.'

The sanctuary was filled with Jews and Christians. The rabbi looked into my eyes and without blinking asked, "What is your deepest prayer for the Jewish people?"

And I almost went into auto-pilot and gave him the Jesus talk.

"What would be so wrong with that?" Christian readers ask.

Think about it.

His question was filled with historic horror as well as future hope, warranting much more consideration than the answer he was fully expecting to hear from me-- an answer confirming his suspicions that nothing had really changed in Christianity's perception of the Jews.

"Rabbi, let me tell you a story," I suggested.

The Saban Leadership Seminar

In 2006 I was invited to speak at the AIPAC Saban Leadership Seminar, the organization's premier student political leadership training seminar. This biannual event is presented through AIPAC's Schusterman Advocacy Institute, and held in Washington, D.C. More than three hundred of AIPAC's top student activists from over one hundred campuses participate in three days of intense grassroots political and advocacy training. During this seminar, students meet with top Washington policymakers, elected officials and Middle East experts.

The wrap-up banquet I was asked to address happened to fall on my daughter Sterling's thirteenth birthday. Before answering the request from AIPAC, I told her about the speaking invitation, and reminded her that she was more important to me than anything else in the world.

"Sweetheart, I can call AIPAC and explain to them there is no way I can be there for the event, or I can go to D.C. and we'll celebrate your birthday when I get home," I offered her.

"NO, DAD!" my precious Zionist daughter scolded me. "You need to go, and we can have my birthday later," she assured me with a big smile.

"But-- you really owe me." Her smile appeared to grow slightly menacing.

Jewish College Student Activists

From the giddiness in the atmosphere of the beautiful D.C. Hilton Hotel lobby, I could tell that the hundreds of pro-Israel college students had really been energized by the Saban Seminar. I had been moved to tears of concern numerous times in my preparation to speak, and my apprehension was magnified as the event approached. AIPAC asked me to fill an hour, which is a very long time for anyone to listen to me; and although they had knowingly invited a Christian preacher to speak, I knew I was not there to preach.

What was I to do?

I was seated at the banquet with a table full of students who could not have been kinder or more engaging, and my troubled heart began to calm. Before I could eat my dessert, the Master of Ceremonies whisked me to the stage and my long hour began.

There are rare moments during gatherings such as this where every individual becomes a part of the whole. No longer is a speaker addressing listeners; rather, the engagement becomes a conversation with an assembly of passionate participants. That evening we experienced such a metamorphosis, during which I began to comprehend that the majority of Jewish students in attendance were not the least bit religious.

"What happened at that moment in this gathering would be my prayerful answer to the question you asked," I told the rabbi.

You Are A Jew!

"Pastor Victor," the Jewish college student addressed me as he stood. "It is very, very hard to be a Jew on any college campus and to try to stand for Israel," he bemoaned a painful truth.

Following his statement with a question every student wanted answered, he asked, "Do you have any suggestions on what we can do?"

My response was immediate, unprepared, and seemed to fly out of my mouth like a dove protecting her nest.

"YOU ARE A JEW!!" I exclaimed with tears filling my eyes. "You are the firstborn of HaShem! Yours is the adoption as sons, the Divine Glory, the covenants, the receiving of the Law, the Temple worship and the promises! [from Romans 9:3-5]

"Be strong, be encouraged, do not be terrified, do not be discouraged: for 'HaShem your God is with you wherever you go!' [from Joshua 1:9]

"You are a Jew, and if you can't make it to synagogue yet, your rabbis will understand-- but you have to read your Bible. Until you do, you don't fully know who you are, nor do you know the power of your God! You must read the account of creation and your heritage in God's promise to Abraham recorded in the Book of Genesis, your birth as a slave-child nation and your redemption in the Book of Exodus. You might want to skip Leviticus for a while-- and nobody really likes math, so leave the Book of Numbers until you connect with a rabbi-- but you must also study the Prophets and the Writings! Read your Bible, seek the God of Abraham, Isaac, and Jacob, and *be Jews.* That is what you need to do on your college campuses."

Answering the question:

"What is your deepest prayer for the Jewish people?"

My rabbi friend was crying as I finished my story. He went on to tell me how he had left his faith as a young man, and only after his father's death had he returned to the God of his youth.

"My father would have given you every last penny he had to find me and speak those words you spoke to the students," he stated with deep remorse.

"When I say such things to young Jews," he explained, "they just think, 'Oy, he's a rabbi: of course he's going to scold us!'

"But when you, a Christian pastor, say to them..." he couldn't finish the words.

I then answered, "My friend, within that story is my answer to your question. My deepest prayer for you, and the Jewish people, is that you be good Jews. I pray that you continue to seek the God of Abraham, Isaac, and Jacob within the words of Torah, the Prophets, and the Writings."

As a Christian, I believe in every good thing God desires to reveal to our communities. I believe that He will continue to do so through this Holy book. I also believe those who seek Him, find Him.

The Jews have precious promises, made to them by Almighty God.

Upon His Name He has vowed to keep them.

I believe He will.

Epilogue: One Final Story

The 2008 CUFI Summit had just ended. For those of us called to labor within this movement, there had been thoughts before the conference that perhaps Christians United for Israel was over as well. Months of the most baffling and vicious campaign of lies and distortions concerning the religious beliefs of Pastor Hagee had reached a boiling point with Senator John McCain chucking him and CUFI out of the window of his campaign bus.

But what the enemy meant for evil, God used for good.

Though under enormous pressure not to participate in the conference, independent Democratic Senator Joe Lieberman of Connecticut defied critics, stating his bond with Pastor Hagee was even stronger now than it had been before the controversies.

Lieberman received a standing ovation when he quoted Genesis 45:3 to the more than 4,000 attendees at the Washington Convention Center, exclaiming, *"I am your brother, Joseph!"*

He then went on to quote from the New Testament, saying, "I greet you with the greeting Jerusalem gave to Jesus: 'Blessed are you who come in the Name of the Lord!'"

A number of us at our table were soon suffering dehydration from our nearly non-stop, joyful crying!

Dan Gillerman, the outgoing Israeli ambassador to the United Nations, told CUFI that their love for Israel had sustained him during his six years in the post.

Sitting at the table with my wife and me were two brothers who are rabbis: Rabbi Yossi is from New York and Rabbi Moshe is from Italy. Their father is the Chief Chabad Rabbi of Italy, who oversees more than 800 rabbis. They happened to have read David Brog's book *Standing with Israel,* and could not believe what was happening in the United States concerning Christian support for the nation and people of Israel. Rabbi Moshe had flown all night from Italy to Washington just to see if the phenomenon was true.

The Fingerprints of God

I had been asked to be Senator Lieberman's host at the conference, so I spent the first half of the evening in the green room with him and his staff. At one point I mentioned my new friend Rabbi Moshe and his fact-finding journey from Italy.

Senator Lieberman's speechwriter asked incredulously, "Rabbi Moshe Garelik?"

"Yes, do you know of him?" I asked.

"He was my rabbi when I lived in Europe and is one of the best men I have ever known! He is here tonight?" The young staff member could hardly believe what he had just heard.

We ran out of the green room to my table where Rabbi Moshe was seated, and I looked away as they greeted each other in the supernatural and emotional reunion. It was the fingerprints of God.

Rabbi Moshe and his brother, Rabbi Yossi sat at my table for the Night to Honor Israel Gala Banquet that evening. Never touching the kosher food sitting before them, they sat in statue-like fixed wonder with eyes tearing throughout the entire event. A few minutes before the close of the celebration, Rabbi Moshe leaned over and whispered a request for me to accompany him to the parking lot of the building.

"Of course my friend," I responded.

"Is everything alright?" I inquired.

"I must get back to my father," Moshe explained.

"Wait a minute!" I almost demanded. "You're flying back to Italy right now?? You just got here a few hours ago!" I couldn't believe what I thought he was saying.

"I must return and tell my father what I have just seen," my new friend reported as he leapt into the waiting taxi and sped off to the airport.

The Footsteps of Mashiach

A beautiful Israeli woman came over to our table at the end of the Night to Honor Israel celebration and told me the evening was life-changing for her. Speaking with a thick Israeli accent, she explained, "My rabbi teaches that during the Messianic Kingdom all the gentiles will be..." she paused, looking away for a moment and grasping for the English words that would express her heart-- "The Gentiles will be," she continued "in support of us!"

"Be in support of you?" I asked rhetorically.

"In the world to come, the Gentiles will be required to bring sacrifices to Jerusalem and the nations that refuse to do so will have no rain and be judged by God!" I exclaimed, paraphrasing from Zechariah 14: 16-18, *"Ten men will grab the garment of a*

Jew and say, *"Let us go with you, for we have heard that God is with you,"* I confirmed to her, quoting from Zechariah 8:23.

The very next morning I received the following email from Rabbi Moshe and Rabbi Yossi:

Pastor Victor,
Thank you for giving us the opportunity to witness firsthand one of the greatest miracles in our times. While sitting in that room, I could literally hear the footsteps of Mashiach. There is no question in my mind that this is only the beginning and in the future, millions will follow. You're very fortunate to be a part of such a phenomenal event in history.

Another biblical reference for this belief is from the prophet Isaiah:

Isaiah 49:22-23

This is what the Sovereign Lord says; "See, I will beckon to the Gentiles, I will lift up my banner to the peoples; they will bring your sons in their arms and carry your daughters on their shoulders. Kings will be your foster fathers, and their queens your nursing mothers. They will bow down before you with their faces to the ground; they will lick the dust of your feet. Then you will know that I am the Lord; those who hope in me will not be disappointed.

What the Enemy Meant for Evil...

Pastor Hagee introduced several prominent Roman Catholics who attended the event at his invitation, including Bill Donohue of the influential Catholic League. Donohue had been the most vocal critic of statements incorrectly attributed to Hagee and characterized as anti-Catholic.

Weeks before our summit, Pastor Hagee asked to meet face to face with Donohue and the Catholic leadership. Their gathering ended with prayer, thanksgiving, and with Pastor Hagee's receiving their wholehearted endorsement after they allowed him to open the Bible and present what he actually teaches and believes. The result is that CUFI is broadening its tent to include Roman Catholics who are interested in joining with us in our support of Israel.

"What the enemy meant for evil, God has turned into good," Pastor Hagee reported.

Amen.

Join Us Now!

If you have not done so already, join us by going to: www.cufi.org and adding your name and email address to our CUFI Rapid Response Team. We will send you current Middle East updates, notify you of pro-Israel events in your community, and become a vehicle for you to address the leaders of our nation on legislation and Biblically based political matters affecting the nation of Israel.

Baruch HaShem!

For my Christian readers:
Baruch HaShem is Hebrew for: "Praise the Lord!"

With over 1,200,000 members, CUFI is the largest pro-Israel organization in the United States and one of the leading Christian grassroots movements in the world.

Pastor Velvel

Rabbi Mendy told me I needed a Hebrew name. He bowed his head, wrinkled his forehead, stroked his chin, and remained silent for several moments. All of a sudden he looked up with a grin on his face as though he had received a direct message from God and proclaimed with his booming voice, "You are Velvel! You are Pastor Velvel!"

Velvel is Yiddish for "wolf." I tried to explain to my Jewish friend why this was possibly not a great name for me. You can read *the rest of the story* in my next book, "Jews, Gentiles, and the World to Come!" I hope you enjoy the introduction to the book, included in the next few pages.

Jews, Gentiles, and the World to Come

A new book by Pastor/Author Victor L. Styrsky

Available Summer 2013

At the very moment you are reading this sentence, seated at the right hand of Almighty God and interceding on your behalf is Jesus of Nazareth-- and He is Jewish.

Think about it for a moment.

He was raised by Jewish parents, grew up observing Jewish traditions, and became a Jewish rabbi. He died while lifted up on a wooden stake, under a blackened sun and a crudely carved sign identifying Him as "King of the Jews."

During a brief preview of the reign of Messiah found in the book of Revelation, we see an angel identifying this King of the Jews as the *Lion of the Tribe of Judah* and *Root of David*.

The architectural plans of eternity's epicenter, *The New Jerusalem*, reveal twelve foundation stones named after the twelve Apostles-- twelve Jewish Apostles.

The city is entered through any of the twelve gates, each named after one of the twelve tribes-- of Israel.

The Jewish citizens of this world to come are highly revered by the Gentile nations, as prophesied in the book of Zechariah:

Zechariah 8:23

Thus says Jehovah of Hosts: "In those days it shall come to pass that ten men shall take hold out of all the languages of the Gentile, they shall take hold of the skirt of him that is a Jew, saying, 'We will go with you, for we have heard that God is with you!'

If what you are seeing is an *unfamiliar* pattern of Jewish preeminence awaiting us in the days ahead, then you may have been missing one of the most important messages of the entire Bible.

The Jews are a uniquely chosen people-- *and we'd better get used to it!*

Not a bigger-and-better-than people-- but a chosen people. And most importantly, not *were* a chosen people-- but *are* a chosen people. If not, then apparently heaven hasn't received the memo!

While reading these thoughts, should you find yourself immediately rejecting the direction I am attempting to take you in this book, I beg you to first consider what I imagine is one of the foundational verses of your Scriptural argument with me:

Galatians 3:1

There is neither Greek nor Jew, male nor female, slave nor free, for... all are one in Christ."

A common (and perhaps your) interpretation of Galatians 3:1 goes something like this:

Because of the death and resurrection of Jesus Christ, there are no longer any differences between Jews and Gentiles. He has *fulfilled* the Mosaic Law and now "The middle wall of partition between Jew and Gentile has been torn down." (More on this later.)

By this interpretation, the Jews *were* a chosen people, but now we Christians are God's chosen people *exclusively.*

The Jews were in, had a chance, blew it when they didn't recognize Jesus as their Messiah, so-- until they see what we see and believe what we believe about Him-- they are on the outside looking in because God no longer *sees* Jew or Gentile.

God only sees... Christians.

He only has plans for Christians and He only keeps His promises with Christians, and every praiseworthy and prophetic thing He is doing on the earth has to do with Christians.

And all those promises He made to Abraham, Isaac, Jacob and their Jewish descendants?

Sorry, Jews.

They're all ours now because, as Galatians 3:1 teaches us, there is no longer Jew or Gentile: there are only Christians.

Oneness is Not Sameness

So I asked the young pastor (who had just presented this exegesis on Galatians 3) whether he was married.

"Sure am!" he answered with the glee of a newlywed. "My wife and I have been married for almost a year!" he beamed.

"And your wife," I begin to lay my theological snare, "Is she a Christian?"

"Of course she is," he responded, almost indignantly.

"And is she the Senior Pastor in your church?" I wriggle the bait right under his theological nose to be sure he got a good whiff of it.

"No, no: she works in the Sunday School and helps lead up the nursery. We don't believe in women having authority over men in our church," my fellow pastor proclaimed, backed with his full trust in the biblical accuracy of his seminary degree and denominational stance.

I almost felt bad as I was about to slam the door of my trap upon his dear young head.

"And in your home: is your wife the decision-maker of the family?" I inquired.

The young pastor laughed (without guile) at the utter absurdity of my question.

"Of course not, Pastor Victor!" he grinned. "You don't need to worry about us. I am *definitely* the head of our family," he assured me with a Christian-testosterone level worthy of a twenty-something.

"So in your church and in your marriage, though you and your wife are *one in Christ*, you also believe you both continue to have unique, separate and very distinctive roles as male and female?" I pounced.

Of course he does.

When it comes to the *many* differences between men and women outlined within the Bible, the defining of the boundaries varies within denominational religious traditions although the recognition of them is present in all of our churches.

Also listed as "being one in Christ" within the proclamation of Galatians 3:1 are the Christian slave-owner and the Christian slave he owns:

Galatians 3:1-3

There is neither Greek nor Jew, male or female, slave nor free, for all are one in Christ.

The differences between the Christian slave who is bought and sold at will and the Christian slave-owner can be righteously addressed only through the oppressed voice of the slave, but they are profound. Only the plight of ignorance or disease of arrogance would attempt to diminish them.

So with just a cursory examination of this text we must admit that, "being one in Christ" does not mean there are no longer any differences between slave and free or men and women.

So why do many Christians continue to use this verse as a proof text that God no longer views humanity through a Jewish/Gentile paradigm? And if it doesn't mean what you may have thought it meant a few moments ago-- what is Galatians 3:1-3 all about?

Within the *context* of the book of Galatians, a more unbiased and hermeneutically honest understanding of the meaning of these verses has to do with God's saving grace no longer found solely through being Jewish and adhering to the Jewish faith. Christians believe the offer of salvation is now available to all humanity regardless of race, gender, or social status-- all through faith in the person of Jesus Christ.

Thus, when it comes to the offer and gift of salvation, "There is neither Greek nor Jew, male or female, slave nor free, for all are one in Christ."

If you are seeing some cracks within that which you have previously believed concerning this one portion of Scripture-- please consider taking a new look at the other biblical truths presented in, *Jews, Gentiles, and the World to Come!* I believe you may have some wonderful revelations in store for you concerning the place of the Gentiles within the uniqueness of God's call upon the Jewish people and His eternal promises made to them.

. . . to be continued!

For comments or to order your copy of *Jews, Gentiles, and the World to Come!* contact: <u>Victor@CUFI.org</u>

Resources

Ahmadinejad, Mahmoud . "Address to the UN General Assembly, 2007." *www.cfr.org.* Council on Foreign Relations http://www.cfr.org/iran/president-ahmadinejads-address-un-general-assembly-2007/p14305

Ahmed-Ullah, Noreen S. "A Rare Look at Secretive Brotherhood in America," *Chicago Tribune*: September 19, 2004.

Alexander, Y., ed. *The 1988-1989 Annual on Terrorism.* Netherlands: Kluwer Academic Publishers,1990

Allen, Ronald Barclay. *Worship: Rediscovering the Missing Jewel.* Eugene, OR: Wipf & Stock Publishers, 2001.

American Jewish Historical Society. www.ajhs.org

Andryszewski, Tricia. *Communities of the Faithful: American Religious Movements outside the Mainstream.* Bookfield, CT: Millbrook Press, 1997.

Badi, Muhammad. "Sermon: How Islam Confronts the Oppression and Tyranny." Translated at *memri.org.* Middle East Media Research Institute. September 2010.

Baynes, Norman H., ed. *The Speeches of Adolf Hitler: April 1922-August 1939.* New York: Oxford University Press, 1942.

"Benjamin Disraeli." *Britannia: America's Gateway to the British Isles.* http://www.britannia.com/bios/disraeli.html

Blidstein, Gerald J. *Honor thy Father and Mother: Filial Responsibility in Jewish Law and Ethics.* Jersey City, NJ: Ktav Publishing House, 2006.

Carter, Jimmy. *Palestine: Peace Not Apartheid.* New York: Simon & Schuster, 2007.

Chazan, Robert, ed. *Church, State, and Jew in the Middle Ages.* Springfield, NJ: Behrman House, 1980.

Cohn-Sherbok, Dan. *A Concise Encyclopedia of Judaism.* Oxford: One World Publications, 1999.

Dahoah-Halevi,Jonathan. "The Muslim Brotherhood: A Moderate Islamic Alternative to al-Qaeda or a Partner in Global *Jihad*?" *Jerusalem Viewpoints,* Nov. 1, 2007

English Tanach O-E Stone. Brooklyn, NY: Mesorah Publications, 2011.

"Excerpts from the Hamas Charter." *standwithus.org.* Stand with Us, Los Angeles. http://www.standwithus.com/online_booklets/HamasCharter/HamasCharter.pdf

Fairchild, Mary. "Christianity." *About.com.* Study of Global Christianity (CSGC) at Gordon-Conwell Theological Seminary http://christianity.about.com/od/denominations/p/christiantoday.htm

Ginsburg, Mitch. "Rockets Fired, Likely from Sinai, at Israel Community along Egyptian Border." *The Times of Israel.* November 14, 2012. www.timesofisrael.com/mortars-fired-at-israeli-village-along-egyptian-border/

Gold, Dore. "The Muslim Brotherhood and the Egyptian Crisis." *Jerusalem Issues Briefs,* Feb. 2, 2011

"Hezbollah." www.cfr.org. Council on Foreign Relations. http://www.cfr.org/publication/9155

Hier, M. & Brackman, H. "Mel's Passion." *L.A. Times*, June 22, 2003.

"Israel-PLO Recognition (September 9, 1993)." The Jewish Virtual Library. www.jewishvirtuallibrary.org/ jsource/Peace/recogn.html

Kunztel, Mathais. "Jew-Hatred and Jihad: The Nazi Roots of the 9/11 Attack." *The Weekly Standard,* Sept. 17, 2007 archived at: http://www.discoverthenetworks.org/Articles/JewHatred%20and%20Jihad.pdf

Lepre, George. *Himmler's Bosnian Division: The Waffen-SS Handschar Division, 1943-1945.* Atglen, PA: Schiffer Publishing Ltd., 1997

Lewis, James. "Anti-Zionist Christians." www.americanthinker.com. American Thinker. www.americanthinker.com/2005/07/antizionistchristians.html

"A Little Taste of History," MSA-National Website (Archive), http://web.archive.org/web/20060118061004/http://www.msa-national.org/about/history.html (Accessed May 14, 2007)

McCarthy, Andrew C. "Fear the Muslim Brotherhood." *National Review*, Jan. 31, 2011

Meir-Levi, David. "Palestinians: Aggressors, Not Victims." *USA Partisan.* usapartisan,blogspot.com. November 27, 2007.

Merly, Steven. "The Muslim Brotherhood in the United States." *Current Trends,* April 2009

"The Muslim Brotherhood." *www.investigativeproject.org*. The Investigative Project on Terrorism. Emerson, Steven, ed. Updated May 15, 2012. www.investigativeproject.org/documents/misc/135.pdf

"Muslim Students Association." *www.investigativeproject.org*. The Investigative Project on Terrorism. Emerson, Steven, ed. http://www.investigativeproject.org/documents/misc/31.pdf

National Association of Atomic Veterans. www.naav.com

New American Standard Bible. Nashville, TN: Thomas Nelson, 2008.

New International Bible. Nashville, TN: Thomas Nelson, 2008.

New King James Bible. Nashville, TN: Thomas Nelson, 2008.

New Revised Standard Bible. Nashville, TN: Thomas Nelson, 2008.

Occhiogrosso, Peter. *The Joy of Sects: A Spirited Guide to the World's Religious Traditions.* New York: Doubleday, 1996.

"Pavlov's Dog - About". *Nobelprize.org.* 28 Dec 2012 http://www.nobelprize.org/educational/medicine/pavlov/about.html

People of Faith. *PeopleOfFaith.org.uk*

Peterson, Scott. "Waiting for the Rapture in Iran." *The Christian Science Monitor*, December 21, 2005

Pipes, Daniel. "The Mystical Menace of Mahmoud Ahmadinejad." *New York Sun*, January 10, 2006

Poole, Patrick. "Ahmadinejad's Apocalyptic Faith." *Front Page*, August 17, 2006.
http://www.frontpagemag.com/Articles/Read.aspx?GUID=32B294D4-A21C-4095-8D59-1B49230E3F5D

Ryrie, Charles C. *Basic Theology: A Popular Systematic Guide to Understanding Biblical Truth.* Chicago, IL: Moody Publishers, 1999.

The Saban Leadership Seminar. oncampus@aipac.org

Schwartz, Shari, ed. Scapegoat on Trial: The Story of Mendel Beilis. www.judaicaplace: CIS Publications: 1993.

The Simon Wiesenthal Center.
http://motlc.wiesenthal.com/site/pp.asp?c=gvKVLcMVIuG&b=394713

Slater, Elinor and Robert. *Great Jewish Men.* Middle Village, NY: Jonathan David Publishers, 1996.

Snyder, Louis L., *Encyclopedia of the Third Reich.* Da Capo Press, 1994.

Spiro, Ken. "History Crash Course #64: The British Mandate." *Aish.com*.
http://www.aish.com/h/iid/48961161.html

Sproul, R. C. *Essential Truths of the Christian Faith.* Peabody, MA: Tyndale, 1992.

Telushkin, Joseph. "Maimonides/Rambam." Jewish Virtual Library.org. American-Israeli Cooperative Enterprise.
http://www.jewishvirtuallibrary.org/jsource/biography/maimonides.html

Touger, Eliyahu, trans. "The Laws Concerning Moshiach." The Mishneh Torah: Chapters 11-12. Chabad.org. Chabad-Lubavitch Media Center.
http://www.chabad.org/library/article_cdo/aid/682956/jewish/Mishneh-Torah.htm

"U.N. General Assembly 2006." www.worldjewishcongress.org. World Jewish Congress http://www.worldjewishcongress.org/en/iran/showSpeech/id/2

Vaughn, Robert Alfred. *Hours with the Mystics*, 3*rd ed.* (1856. London: Strahan, 1879.

Vidino, Lorenzo. "The Muslim Brotherhood's Conquest of Europe," *Middle East Quarterly,* Winter 2005

Wendell, Charles, trans. *Five Tracts of Hasan al-Banna.* Berkeley: 1978

Wertheimer, Jack. *A People Divided: Judaism in Contemporary America.* Waltham, MA: Brandeis University Press, 1997.

Winkelman, Roy, dir. "A Teacher's Guide to the Holocaust." Florida Center for Instructional Technology, University of South Florida. fcit.usf/edu/holocaust/

Victor Styrsky has been a pastor, music director, and pro-Israel activist for more than 30 years and is the Christians United for Israel, (CUFI) Eastern Regional Coordinator. Pastor Styrsky is a frequent speaker at churches, synagogues, college campuses, conferences and pro-Israel events across the nation. Victor and his wife Marita have lived in the midst of Northern California's largest Sunni Muslim community for over fifteen years and are proud parents and grandparents.